FRIENDS AND SISTERS

FRIENDS AND SISTERS

by

Sandy Asher

LONDON
VICTOR GOLLANCZ LTD
1982

First published in the United States
of America as *Daughters of the Law*

British Library Cataloguing in Publication Data

Asher, Sandy
   [Daughters of the law]. Friends and sisters.
   I. Title   II. Friends and sisters
   813'.54[J]   PZ7

   ISBN 0-575-03124-7

Photoset in Great Britain by
Rowland Phototypesetting Limited, Bury St Edmunds, Suffolk
and printed by St Edmundsbury Press
Bury St Edmunds, Suffolk

For Becky, Lynn and Honey

1

"We've got to do something about the earthquake in Bucharest!" Denise Riley announced. She folded back the newspaper and waved a photo of that devastated city at her mother, who was hunched over a cutting board at the kitchen counter.

Mrs Riley stopped slicing a tomato and rubbed an itch on the tip of her nose with the back of her wrist. Tomato juice dribbled off the knife she still held.

"What?" she asked.

"There's been an earthquake in Bucharest," Denise repeated, rattling the paper in front of her mother's blinking eyes. "It says so right here: *Deerfield Bulletin*, page one. Over five hundred dead. Thousands injured. Little children hurt and homeless. We've got to do something about it."

"Stop waving that thing so I can read," Mrs Riley said. She studied the photograph for a moment, a frown creasing her forehead. Then she shot a puzzled glance towards Denise.

"What exactly did you have in mind?" she asked.

Denise snatched back the paper. "Ah!" she yelped.

"What's wrong?"

"I gave myself a paper cut," Denise muttered, sucking the side of her index finger.

Mrs Riley shook her head and went back to work on her tomato. "Honestly, Pumpkin," she sighed. "You really ought to concentrate on getting yourself through the day unscathed instead of worrying about things you can't do anything about. Have you practised today?"

Denise gave her cut a sullen but thorough inspection. It wasn't bleeding but it certainly did sting.

"Not yet," she muttered.

"You know what Dr Baker said," Mrs Riley warned, giving the tomato an energetic chop for emphasis.

"I know. I've got to practise ballet every day to improve my coordination. But even coordinated people get paper cuts." With lightning speed, Denise whisked a box of croutons off the cutting board.

"Stop that!" her mother commanded. "My God, I almost chopped off your fingers!"

Denise filled one hand with croutons and stuffed some into her mouth.

"I swear," her mother went on, "you'll eat anything that's not nailed down. Dr Baker also said . . ."

"I've got to improve my eating habits," Denise finished, around a mouthful of croutons.

"Or you'll float into your thirteenth birthday like the Goodrich blimp," her mother tacked on.

"Goodyear," Denise corrected her. "How long do I have to go to a paediatrician anyway?"

"Dr Baker will let us know."

"I hate sitting in that waiting room with all those *children*."

"Practise ballet, eat properly, and you won't have to."

Denise groaned and headed towards her father's study, a converted large alcove off the living room. On the way, she bumped her hip against a dining room chair, knocking it off balance. Reaching out to save the chair, she dropped the newspaper. Gathering up the newspaper, she brought her head up on the underside of the table with a sickening crunch. A quick glance back at her mother revealed exactly what she'd expected: Mrs Riley wore an I-told-you-so

8

smirk. She waved the knife at Denise as an added incentive to practise, a playful gesture, but firm.

Without further damage to herself or the furniture, Denise arrived at her father's study. There she tucked the paper under her arm and rapped lightly on the door.

"Yeah? What? What is it?" came her father's muffled response.

"It's me, Daddy," Denise called.

Mr Riley opened the door and peered out, one long arm stretched to the doorknob, his swivel chair straining, ready to dump him out backwards if he forced its springs one more inch.

"Yeah, Pumpkin? What? Is dinner ready?"

"No, not yet. May I come in?"

Mr Riley sighed. "I'm right in the middle of something. Is it important?"

"Yes, it's important. There's been an earthquake in Bucharest," Denise informed him, "and I've been wondering what we're going to do about it."

Mr Riley let go of the doorknob and let the chair spring twang him into an upright position. He removed his horn-rimmed glasses and placed them gently on his desk. With the thumb and index finger of his right hand, he massaged the bridge of his nose, making three tiny, deliberate circles. His eyes were squeezed shut. Denise shifted from one foot to the other uncomfortably. Finally, Mr Riley spoke, his voice weary, his words meted out slowly and with painstaking precision.

"Pumpkin," he said, "I have an important meeting about this grant proposal at nine o'clock tomorrow morning. I have, by conservative estimate, twenty hours of work left to do on it before then. It is now approximately six p.m., give or take a quarter of an hour. Simple mathematical calculation will tell you that I cannot be bothered with such nonsense."

"Nonsense? Daddy! It's an *earthquake*! Over seven-point-

9

zero on the Richter scale. Blocks of ten- and twelve-storey buildings *flattened*. Ten thousand people *homeless*."

"It's going to be ten thousand and three if I don't get this grant."

"Daddy, you know we won't be homeless if . . ."

Mr Riley's eyes flashed an icy blue. His voice took on a sharp edge. "Pumpkin, I have work to do."

"Okay," Denise grunted and backed out of the office. Like a giant's slap, the door swung shut in her face. With an angry shake of her dishevelled red curls, she stomped upstairs and flopped back on her bed, the newspaper clutched to her chest as she stared at the ceiling. It wasn't right, she thought, to make a kid do current events assignments. You found out the whole world was going to pieces: earthquakes, terrorist bombings, sky-jackers, pollution, energy shortages, muggers. You name it, somebody somewhere was suffering from it. And then you found out nobody was going to *do* anything about it. They all just went right on with their lives, slicing tomatoes, massaging their noses. Even Mrs Gaston, her social studies teacher. All *she* ever did was tack the newspaper clippings on a notice board. How did that ever help any starving kid in India, having an article tacked to a stupid notice board? Nobody ever read a single one of those articles anyway, except the kid who brought it in. Maybe. Most of the time, that kid only read the headline and the caption under the photograph—just enough to write a dumb little report.

Denise rolled onto her side and opened the drawer in her night table. She pulled out a sheet of paper, folded in thirds. It was a letter she'd read and reread, folded and refolded. The fine stationery was inscribed, "U.S. House of Representatives."

"Dear Miss Riley," she read, for at least the hundredth time. "Thank you for your letter and your interest in the issues of gun control, nuclear disarmament, solar energy, and the population explosion. I would like to take this opportunity to express my gratitude for your support and to let you know your opinions will most certainly be given careful consideration. Very sincerely yours, Walter H. Huffnagle, Representative, 213th District."

Denise read the letter through twice, sighed deeply, and tossed it back into the drawer. She'd been so excited when that letter first arrived. She'd danced all over the house, crowing, "He wrote to me! He's going to give my opinions careful consideration!" Then her father had come home from his lab, glanced at the letter and guffawed. "Huffnagle's been writing that same letter for twenty-seven years," he'd said. He'd ruffled Denise's coppery curls and gone in to the living room. "You know what, Natalie?" he'd said to Mrs Riley, "I'll bet Huffnagle died years ago. I'll bet you anything there's just a machine in that mouldy office of his, turning out those letters day after day!"

Then, as now, Denise had retreated to her room. It wasn't fair, she thought. Nobody listened. Nobody did anything. By the time she grew up, the world wouldn't be fit to live in. "The price of liberty is eternal vigilance," somebody famous had said. Ben Franklin, maybe? Thomas Jefferson? Somebody *heroic*. Somebody who *did* things.

Suddenly, Denise sat up straight, swung her legs over the side of the bed, and opened the drawer wider. Separating layers of theatre programmes, birthday cards, newspaper clippings, and other debris, she fished out a red spiral notebook. The notebook was divided into three sections. Each section had a heading written on a tab: WRITE TO. DO. LEARN MORE ABOUT.

The WRITE TO section was the thinnest. Many pages had been torn out as letters were drafted to congressmen, senators, Dear Abby, and various stars of TV and screen. Few of the letters ever got an answer. That was why Representative Huffnagle had been such a triumph, until . . .

11

Denise passed over the WRITE TO section, turning instead to LEARN MORE ABOUT. There was a list of several dozen items. Some, like "Abortion," had lines drawn through them. Others, like "Treatment of American Indians," apparently still needed to be dealt with. Under the last entry, "Nuclear Breeder-Reactors" (not crossed out), Denise added "Earthquakes." After a pause, she scribbled in "Bucharest—find out where?" and "Richter scale—what?" Contemplating what she had written for a moment, she found it satisfactory and moved on to the DO section, feeling as if she were accomplishing something already. Under DO, she consulted a long list of possibilities. She passed over "Picket" and "Write letter," but hesitated thoughtfully beside the next suggestion. Then, with a burst of enthusiasm, she dropped her pen, found it in the creases of her bedspread, and drew two—no, *three*—bold lines under her selection: "Stage hunger strike."

"Bill? Pumpkin? Dinner's ready!" Mrs Riley called from the bottom of the stairs. Right on cue, Denise thought. She stashed her notebook away in its drawer and lay back on her bed again.

"Pumpkin? Wash your hands. Dinner's ready."

Denise folded her arms across her chest, clenched her teeth, and said nothing.

"Denise Riley, are you alive up there? Answer me!"

Denise bit her lip.

Her mother's footsteps shuffled up the stairs. "Denise, did you hear me? What is *wrong* with you?" Mrs Riley's concerned face appeared in the doorway. Denise quickly looked away and focused on a wispy cobweb dangling in a corner of the ceiling.

"Why are you lying there like that?"

"I'm staging a protest."

"A protest? What for? I mean, what against?"

"I'm not going to eat until you do something about the earthquake in Bucharest."

"Oh, no, not that again."

Tears made the cobweb wriggle, then slid down Denise's freckled cheeks and into her ears. She let them slide.

"You never do anything about anything," she insisted. "This time I'm not going to just forget about it."

"Oh, come on, Pumpkin. We feel sorry for the people in Bucharest. But we really can't do anything for them. We do donate blood to the Red Cross, you know. Daddy and I both do. And the Red Cross is over there, I'm sure, doing what they can. But terrible things happen every day all over the world. We can't possibly cope with everything. It's all we can do to take care of ourselves most of the time."

"We have plenty of food, plenty of clothing. We own a house," Denise said.

"The Deerfield Savings and Loan Association owns this house, if you want to know the truth," Mrs Riley explained, her voice rising slightly as her patience wore thinner. "We just pay the mortgage. And the taxes. And the insurance. And that's about all we can handle right now, if you don't mind."

"You don't even *try*," Denise insisted. "Maybe there wouldn't be so many terrible things if people would just *try*."

Just then, Mr Riley's voice boomed up the stairwell.

"Natalie? Didn't you call us for dinner?"

"Yes, I'll be right there."

"Let's get it over with, huh? I've got to get back to work."

Mrs Riley threw Denise a last exasperated look and disappeared, her sandals clackety-clacking down the stairs.

"Where's Pumpkin?" Denise heard her father ask.

"She's not eating," came her mother's reply.

"Well, that's a switch. Why not? Is she sick?"

"She's staging a hunger strike."

"What?"

13

"A hunger strike, a *protest*. She's not going to eat until we help the earthquake victims in Budapest."

"*Bucharest!*" Denise bellowed.

"Oh, for Pete's sake," she heard her father say. "Pumpkin Riley, you get down here. You get down here this instant or you'll have no allowance for a month. Do you hear me?"

Denise flipped over and buried her face in her pillow.

"Oh, Bill, leave her alone. She'll eat later. Or sooner. How long can she go without food? Ten minutes? Fifteen, tops."

"She's interrupted my work, my dinner, and my peace of mind," Mr Riley roared. "Really, Natalie, this is too much. What does she want us to do, fly to Bucharest and administer mouth-to-mouth resuscitation? *Pumpkin, you get down here!*"

Denise heard her mother giggle. "Come on, Bill. Let's eat. Your fish is getting cold. C'mon. C'mon, c'mon, c'mon."

"Natalie! Stop that!"

Denise knew her mother was tickling her father's ribs. That's what she always did when he worked too hard and got all tense and overwrought, as she called it. Usually, Denise jumped into the fray and they all ended up rolling on the floor and screaming with laughter. But not this time. Denise sucked in her breath and listened.

"C'mon, c'mon, c'mon."

"Oh, ha, ha, ha, ha. Natalie! Quit it! Hoo, hoo, hoo."

The sounds of their tussling faded towards the dining room. After a while, glasses and silverware could be heard clinking. Then a few muffled words and Mr Riley's study door closed. The kitchen taps ran, dishes scraped and clunked together, the water stopped.

The sun sank.

Finally, Denise got out of bed, feeling stiff and heavy from lying so still. As she was changing into her pyjamas,

14

her mother arrived, carrying a tray with a glass of milk and a peanut butter and banana sandwich on it.

"Sorry you missed out on the mackerel," she said. Denise went on buttoning her pyjama top and pretending not to hear her.

"You've got to eat something," her mother went on. "I'll just leave this here, okay?" Mrs Riley brushed a kiss across Denise's cheek. Denise could smell the faint fishy aroma on her breath. Oh, mackerel. Denise adored mackerel. Her stomach growled a long, deep complaint.

"Go on and eat, Pumpkin," Mrs Riley urged. Then she left, closing the door behind her.

The smell of peanut butter and banana filled the room. Denise's stomach scolded her furiously. It felt as if it were being sucked inside out. Denise considered putting the tray out in the hall, but decided that would only bring her mother back to argue with her. So she got a book off her desk, *The Secret of the Hidden Chamber*, and climbed into bed with it. She fluffed up her pillow, propped it against the headboard, and began to read.

"May Elizabeth Wooster gazed up fearfully at the huge man blocking her exit."

Five minutes later, May Elizabeth Wooster was still gazing up fearfully at the huge man blocking her exit. Denise had been reading the same sentence over and over while her mind wrestled with her stomach over the peanut butter and banana sandwich. She moaned and slammed the book shut. Then, before she had time to reconsider, the sandwich sprang from the tray to her hand to her mouth. And was gone. The milk chased after it in one long, greedy gulp.

Not until then did she notice the slip of paper tucked under the sandwich plate. Brushing crumbs off her pyjamas, she read:

"Pumpkin, I don't know where this prayer comes from, but I thought it might help: 'God, grant me the courage to change the things I can change, the serenity to accept those I cannot change, and the wisdom to know the difference.' Love, Mom.''

What in the world was *that* supposed to mean?

2

The house seemed to have given up. Like the late September afternoon, it appeared hopeless, a worn-out, lifeless thing, waiting for winter. Ruthie Morgenthau examined the small, sagging porch, half-drawn blinds, and scraggly front lawn. They resembled the mouth, eyes, and unkempt beard of a person who had lost interest in life, a tramp shuffling down some alleyway with nowhere to go and nothing to care about anymore. Ruthie shuddered. As soon as I get my sketchbook unpacked, she told herself, I'll draw it like that.

She hurried back to her Aunt Sarah's car, where her mother and aunt were engaged in one of their anxious whispering conferences. As always, it stopped as soon as Ruthie drew closer.

"I know it doesn't look like much," Aunt Sarah chirped, bobbing around to open the car boot. Neatly packed into a turquoise jump suit, she looked like a chubby, excited bluejay.

"It's fine," Ruthie's mother replied, a tired, sombre grey dove by comparison.

Aunt Sarah's mascaraed blue eyes appeared from behind the open boot, bleary with tears. "It's not fine, Hannah. We both know it's not fine. But you won't let me help you and . . ."

"It's fine," Mrs Morgenthau repeated, her tone flat and distant, as if she were talking to herself. Her veiled hazel eyes avoided Aunt Sarah's pleading face, swept over the gloomy house, and landed on Ruthie.

17

"Help with the suitcases," she asked softly.

"Sure, Mama," Ruthie said and began to lug one of the battered brown cases out of the gaping boot. When she turned back towards the house, her mother was standing in the middle of the cracked path, her hands loosely clasped before her, a faraway expression on her face. Ruthie turned away quickly, busying herself with the suitcase. Aunt Sarah cleared her throat, then smiled determinedly and climbed the steps to open the front door. Mrs Morgenthau remained where she was.

Ruthie gagged as she followed Aunt Sarah into the house. Everything smelled musty. She became conscious of a faint sour odour of cats. Was all of Deerfield like this? Ruthie wondered. The ride from the bus depot had revealed a long line of petrol stations, discount stores, flea markets and blocks of dreary bungalows like this one. But Aunt Sarah drove a beautiful blue Lincoln Continental. Surely she didn't live in a place like this.

Ruthie was gazing out of a streaked bedroom window at the narrow, weed-choked yard when Aunt Sarah called her into the kitchen. Crossing the living room, she found her mother seated stiffly on the thick maroon sofa, still gazing blankly into space.

"Mama, are you okay?"

The only answer was a slight, almost imperceptible nod. Anyone else would probably have missed it, but Ruthie was used to searching for hints and clues to her mother's odd changes of mood. She'd lived with them all her life, the mysterious. nods, silences, and screams. They were more important and meaningful, somehow, than ordinary conversation. Timidly, she touched her mother's shoulder, then continued on into the kitchen.

Immediately, Aunt Sarah pulled her to the farthest corner.

"You'll make her come to my house for dinner tonight," she whispered up into Ruthie's face. Even though Ruthie was small for a twelve-year-old, she was already two inches taller than her tiny, plump aunt. They were huddled so closely now, Ruthie could see dark roots peeking through Aunt Sarah's carefully curled silver hair and fine lines crisscrossing her cheeks and forehead under the powder. Aunt Sarah was well over sixty, but she looked forty-five, if you didn't get too close, and she had the energy of a young girl.

Now she encircled Ruthie's arm with her pudgy hand. The hard, long nails glistened silvery white in the cold afternoon sun slanting through the windows over the sink.

"Look at you," she went on. "You're skinny as a rail. Doesn't she feed you? Don't you eat?"

"I eat, Aunt Sarah. I'm just skinny. I've always been skinny."

"Well, it's no good. You're a growing girl. You need vitamins, minerals, or you'll get taller and taller and skinnier and skinnier. You'll look like a beanpole."

Ruthie smiled. Aunt Sarah was so different from Ruthie's mother. She was bright and funny, a little frantic sometimes and often insistent, but under all the noise and glitter, she was kind, loving, and lovable. She was different from her brother, too, Ruthie's father. Although they were both very strong-willed, Aunt Sarah's energy sprang from her never-ending good cheer, while Ruthie's father's forcefulness had always seemed propelled by rage.

"She's been worse since . . ." Aunt Sarah began, almost reading Ruthie's mind.

Ruthie nodded. Since Papa died, she finished silently. Here was the latest thing not to be discussed, the latest in a line that stretched back as long as she could remember. The list included God, her parents lives before they'd come to America, and now, death. In the two months since her father's fatal heart attack, she and her mother had almost stopped talking to each other entirely.

19

"I suppose that's to be expected," Aunt Sarah went on. "But I wish she would let me help her more. I don't understand it. Do you know what it is? Is it pride? Or what?"

"I don't know," Ruthie admitted. There was so much, *so much* she didn't know about her mother that sometimes she felt a hole deep inside her growing wider and deeper as if it would one day swallow her alive.

Suddenly, without turning, Ruthie felt her mother's presence in the room.

"So," Mrs Morgenthau said, her tone lighter, as if nothing unusual had happened, "a little cleaning up and it won't be too bad." She ran a finger over the green counter and examined it for dust. "Not too bad."

"Hannah, you'll come to my house for dinner tonight, you and Ruthie."

"Oh, no, Sarah, please. You've done enough."

"Mama, Aunt Sarah wants to welcome us to Deerfield. It's rude to say no. Another time, we'll invite her here. We'll pay her back."

"You don't have . . ." Aunt Sarah began, but Ruthie shot her a warning glance and she changed her approach. "Of course, you'll pay me back. In fact, I'm paying *you* back. How many times did I come to Boston and you fed me? Twenty? Thirty? A hundred? I owe you an invitation, Hannah."

Mrs Morgenthau sighed and opened the refrigerator. Immediately, Aunt Sarah hopped back into action, chattering as she rummaged through its contents. "I put in a little milk, butter, a loaf of bread, a little cheese, some fruit. You shouldn't have to shop right away. A little cereal is in the cupboard. Ruthie, you like Cheerios?"

Ruthie nodded, grinning. There was no keeping her aunt down. Like an underground spring, if you stopped her in one place, she just bubbled up somewhere else.

"But this is for tomorrow," Aunt Sarah went on.

"Tonight it's my house. And a drive around your new town before it gets too dark. So? It's settled."

Smiling in spite of herself, Mrs Morgenthau agreed.

As if given permission now to do anything and everything, Aunt Sarah led the way in unpacking suitcases, then bustled her two charges out the door and back into the car.

The road south to Aunt Sarah's house led through the centre of Deerfield, a clean square with shops and offices, small and undistinguished compared to Boston, but pleasant enough. Not far from the square Aunt Sarah pointed out the public library and then a large red brick building.

"That's your new school, Ruthie. Gardner Junior High. I've already announced your arrival and I'll take you in tomorrow morning, if you want. Or maybe you'd rather go yourself? Not so much like a kindergarten baby, huh?"

"I guess I can go by myself," Ruthie answered, eyeing the building. It didn't look much different from her old school. But it made her feel nervous and shy. Her eyelids fluttered as if trying to block out the sight.

"It's centrally located," Aunt Sarah babbled on, "so it draws kids from several sections of the city. Deerfield is very strange. It's divided up like a patchwork quilt, or like Oz, into little kingdoms. Northwest, where you are, is mostly not so well-off. People from farms that failed who came into the city to find work. In the northeast, they're rich and they're poor and they're everything in between, but they're also black. Our own ghetto. Although why call it that? All the others are in ghettos, too! In the southwest, it's nice, middle-class, and they all hope to move to the southeast—which is where I am—our own Park Avenue with the doctors and the lawyers and the widows of jewellers like myself. *Alevesholim*, may my Izzy rest in peace. Anyway, Gardner is nice, because you get a little sample from each kingdom."

The streets began to twist and meander through rows of

tall maple trees and soon the flat identical tracts of ranch houses gave way to individually styled and landscaped two- and three-storey houses. To Ruthie, they looked like mansions, except that mansions around Boston had a lot more land to them, often fields with grazing horses. These houses were close together, some of them looming so large on their plots they resembled elephants cramped into fenced pens.

Aunt Sarah swerved the car into a driveway that curved up to a white colonial two-storey house with columns soaring from the porch to the roof. "Here we are," she announced, hopping out of the car and leading the way like a drum majorette at the head of a parade.

Ruthie was open-mouthed with awe as Aunt Sarah marched them from room to beautiful room. Her fingers twitched with longing to sketch the graceful furniture and tall latticed windows. Mrs Morgenthau followed, last in line, shaking her head as if it were all too much to believe.

"So? What do you think?" Aunt Sarah asked, halting the parade in the dining room, where three bowls of soup were already waiting for them.

"It's really something," Mrs Morgenthau admitted.

"It's beautiful, Aunt Sarah," Ruthie said.

"You bet," Aunt Sarah agreed, taking her seat at the head of the table and snapping out her napkin. "And believe me, we deserve it. We worked like dogs for it. My Izzy worked himself to death, may God rest his soul."

Ruthie bowed her head over the soup and spooned up a mouthful. It was golden and thick with chicken and noodles. It tasted wonderful. She thought about her parents, who also "worked like dogs," spending hours in the shop below their apartment, altering and tailoring clothes. Why were they never proud and content like Aunt Sarah and Uncle Izzy?

The rest of the meal, a delicious pot roast with carrots and potatoes, was served on a silver platter by an elderly woman named Maybelle who kidded Aunt Sarah as if she were an old friend rather than a servant.

"Maybelle has been with me over twenty years," Aunt Sarah explained. "She fusses at me worse than a mother."

While they were waiting for dessert, Aunt Sarah leaned back in her chair, belched softly and announced:

"So? It's all settled. Come June, Ruthie will have her Bat Mitzvah and I will give such a party like Deerfield has never seen."

"What?" Ruthie gasped, looking from her aunt to her mother in surprise. Mrs Morgenthau said nothing.

"It's the least I can do for my only brother's only child. And my godchild, I might add. I've already spoken to Rabbi Davis and you can start your Hebrew lessons whenever you're ready. The sooner the better, of course."

"Mama?"

Mrs Morgenthau continued to stare at the lacey table-cloth, one gnarled finger brushing crumbs into a neat hill in front of her. "We'll see," she said, softly. "Excuse me, please."

Before anyone could speak, she was out of her chair and on her way to the cloakroom across the hall. Ruthie sat stiffly until she heard the lock click.

"Aunt Sarah, what is this all about?"

"You're a Jewish girl and you will be thirteen next spring. It's time for your bat mitzvah."

"But we don't . . . Papa never . . . we don't even go to synagogue. Ever."

"Then maybe it's time you began. At thirteen, you're an adult in the eyes of the congregation. You have to choose for yourself. Wouldn't you like to know what it is you're choosing or not choosing? Wouldn't you like to go to Hebrew school?"

"I don't know."

"It's an honour to read from the Torah at your bat mitzvah. And a duty, too. If it's your mother you're worried about, don't concern yourself. I'll convince her, just leave it to me. So? It's all arranged, huh?"

Ruthie clapped her hands over her ears as a rush of conflicting, confusing thoughts crowded her head.

"I don't know, Aunt Sarah," she said. "Please let me think it over, okay? Please?"

3

With her chin bobbing on top of her loose-leaf notebook, Denise watched her sneakers trudge towards school. Kick-kick, flap-flap. That and the whoosh-whoosh of her jean legs slapping against each other were all she noticed. Except for the cold wind slamming her sideways at each corner. You could hardly miss that. Autumn. Phooey. Monday. Nuts. *School*. Yuck. Occasionally another body trotted past, a voice called, "Hi!" But Denise ignored everything and everyone outside her own miserable self. Kick-kick, flap-flap, whoosh-whoosh, slam!

Not only had she failed at last night's hunger strike, but when her father threatened to cut off her allowance for twenty years if she didn't eat breakfast, she'd gobbled up three bowls of cereal. *Three bowls!* Her mother had found the whole episode absolutely hilarious and had laughed so hard, she'd spluttered coffee all over the tablecloth. As parents went, they were really idiotic sometimes. How could they laugh when people all over the world were suffering? How *could* they?

Denise watched the rubber tips of her sneakers shuffle to a stop at the curb. Quickly, stealthily, she glanced at the traffic light. It was green. She fastened her eyes to her shoes once more and proceeded.

"Hopeless!" she snorted under her breath. "The whole world is hopeless. The human race is a wreck and we should all hurl ourselves off the planet. So why am I going to school?"

She'd been forced to go, physically coerced. Her parents had each taken an elbow and hustled her out the door, much to their own amusement. She knew they were trying to jolly her out of her mood. Well, she had no intentions of being jollied.

The pavement beneath her rubber soles turned lighter in colour and smoother, then gave way to schoolyard. Several strides later, she mounted concrete stairs and stepped onto wooden floor. After dumping her windbreaker in her locker, she slumped into Room 112 and sank into her seat. She put her head down on top of the books piled on her desk. She would have preferred lying on the floor. Or better yet, burrowing under the foundation, along with the other worms. She was that low.

I will not speak to another living soul for a year, she decided. A month, she redecided. Except teachers, if they speak to me first, she decided for the third and absolutely final time.

She was aware of a body sliding into the seat in front of hers. A lilac odour wafted her way. That would be Maxine Fitzhugh.

"Well, I was lying with my head on his lap, see, and whenever he wanted to kiss me, he just kind of rolled me back and leaned over."

"Oh, wow," said a second voice to Denise's right. A strong soapy smell enveloped the lilacs. That would be Betsy Williamson. Betsy always looked scrubbed to within an inch of her life. She was battling an acne problem, Betsy was, valiantly but without much success.

Maxine continued: "So I had to take my earring off, see, on that side, because it hurt when I rolled on it. And then my Mom wanted to know, when I got home, how come I only had on one earring."

"Oh, wow," said Betsy.

Denise pressed a hand over her exposed ear. If there was anything she didn't need just then, it was to listen to Maxine

26

Fitzhugh wow Betsy Williamson with her sex life. Maxine was the crown princess of Homeroom 112, maybe even of the entire seventh grade. Or the whole school. Or the whole world, maybe. What did it matter? She was, in Denise's considered opinion, an unearthly creep who cared more about who pierced whose ears than about civil rights or world hunger. Denise had taken an instant dislike to her during the first five minutes of the school year and had since found no reason to change her mind. The feeling was apparently mutual. Rejected by Maxine, Denise found herself ignored by the rest of the class as well. So what? Who cared? Certainly not she. They were *all* creeps. No redeeming virtues whatsoever, as far as she could tell, with the possible exception of Todd Jones, whose five-foot-nine-inch height mercifully kept Denise from being the tallest person in the class.

Denise did have to admit, however, that Maxine Fitzhugh was very well developed for her age, not in height, but in proportions. Like the wind at every corner, you could hardly miss it. Maxine wore a size 32B bra and had gone to great pains on the first day of school to make sure everyone knew that. Denise did not appreciate the information. She, herself, did not wear a bra at all. First of all, most women worth their salt had already burned their bras. And second of all, she would have been stuck with a *training* bra like Betsy's. The very thought made her gag. Wearing a training bra was like wearing one of those signs builders put up on empty lots: "This is the future site of Mammary Towers, another beautifying project of the Estrogen Development Corporation." Any fool could see that that was why Maxine let Betsy tag along with her wherever she went: it made Maxine look that much better by comparison.

And just in case somebody somewhere still failed to notice just how well Maxine's body was shaping up, she wore T-shirts with messages printed across the front, like "Smile!" and "Dynamite!"

27

Even with her ear covered, Denise could hear Maxine whispering at full volume. Betsy Williamson squealed and snorted appropriately at all the dramatic pauses, often spritzing in her excitement. Betsy salivated like a dog when she got emotional, which was nearly always. For all her medicated soap, Denise mused, Betsy Williamson was unsanitary.

"So I told her I thought my ear was getting infected."

"Ooooh, tssss, tsss, tsssssss, that was quick thinking. But didn't she *look*?"

"Sure."

"Oh, wow! What did she say?"

"She said, 'Hmmmmm. Yes, it does seem a bit red for some reason.'"

"Ooooh, tssss, hoo, hoo, hoo, tssss! Do you think he'll call you again?"

"He . . . Oh, my God. What's that?"

"Huh? Oh!"

Even Denise had to look up to see what Betsy and Maxine were gawking at. A silence had fallen over the rest of the class and everyone's eyes were trained on the doorway.

There was a girl huddled there, the strangest kid Denise had ever seen. It wasn't her clothes. They were ordinary jeans and a red plaid shirt. They looked brand new. It wasn't her hair, either, which hung to her shoulders in thick, dark curls. But she was so small and *skinny*. And her huge brown eyes looked *terrified*, almost ready to spill over with tears. Oddest of all, her skin was unbelievably pale, as if she'd been living at the back of a cave, like a mushroom. She stayed frozen there, beside the doorway, with everyone staring at her, until Mrs Gaston breezed in right past her. Three or four steps into the room, Mrs Gaston stopped and whirled around.

"Oh, hello there. I almost didn't see you. Might you be Ruth Morgenthau?"

The girl nodded, her eyes blinking rapidly.

28

"Oh, good!" Mrs Gaston gushed. "Welcome to Home-room 112, Ruth. Is it Ruth or do you prefer a nick-name?"

"Ruthie."

"Everyone, this is Ruthie Morgenthau. She just moved to Deerfield from . . . from?" She glanced at the new girl for help. Ruthie murmured something.

"What did she say?" Maxine demanded. Echoes and snickers ricocheted around the room.

"Speak up, please, Ruthie," Mrs Gaston chirped, her sweet smile going slightly sour.

"Boston," the new girl offered. It seemed to cost her all her energy to get it out.

"Boston!" Mrs Gaston cried, perking right up again. "Ruthie comes from Boston," she told the class. "How marvellous! We've just finished a unit on the American Revolution, haven't we, class?"

"Yeeeeeeessssssss," everyone wailed. Except Denise, who couldn't take her eyes off the new girl. How unhappy she looked! How helpless and lonely. And yet, there was something very sweet and gentle about her, too. Denise's heart went out to her.

". . . someone volunteer to guide Ruthie through her schedule for the first few days?" Mrs Gaston was saying.

Denise's hand shot into the air.

"I will! I will!" she cried.

"It figures," she heard Maxine mutter. Betsy's spritz followed right on cue, but Denise didn't care.

"Thank you, Denise," Mrs Gaston cooed. "That's so kind of you. Denise Riley will be our official hostess, class, but I do hope we will all try our very best to make Ruthie feel welcome. Ruthie, why don't you take that empty seat next to Denise?"

The new girl shuffled down the aisle towards Denise, gnawing on her lower lip. The second she passed Maxine, Maxine rolled her eyes heavenwards and the signal travelled around the room faster than Morse Code. Ruthie was *not* approved of by the Princess.

Denise gritted her teeth, more determined than ever to befriend this Ruthie Morgenthau. Anyone Maxine disliked had to have *something* going for her.

"Hi," Denise offered as Ruthie sat down beside her.

Ruthie didn't even look up.

Mrs Gaston read the day's announcements and then let the class talk softly until the bell rang. Denise was aware of the furtive glances and snickers directed towards the new girl. But Ruthie was apparently aware of nothing but her own frail little hands twisting in her lap.

"My name's Denise Riley," Denise tried again, immediately blushing under her freckles. "I guess you know that already. Mrs Gaston mentioned it."

"I'm Ruthie," the new girl murmured, still concentrating on her hands, frowning at them as if they were annoying her in some way.

Denise noticed a sketchbook peering out from underneath Ruthie's loose-leaf notebook.

"Are you taking art lessons?" she asked.

Ruthie shook her head, no. A hand flew up and tucked the sketchbook under the notebook, then fluttered back into her lap.

Denise sighed. The bell rang.

"Ruthie," Mrs Gaston called over the shuffling of feet and books, "if you have any pictures of Boston's historical landmarks, we'd be so delighted if you'd share them with us."

A slight nod was the only sign Ruthie gave that she'd heard Mrs Gaston. But all through the morning, sitting next to her in maths and English, Denise watched in wonder as Ruthie covered page after page in her sketchbook with what had to be pictures of Boston's historical sights. She worked frantically, ignoring everything else, as if she had to capture every inch of Boston before social studies

30

class on penalty of death. At the lunch table, she forgot to eat. She just went on working, with her sketchbook in her lap and her head bent practically under the table.

"She didn't mean you had to share pictures of Boston *today*," Denise told her. "And she probably meant photographs anyway."

Ruthie went on sketching. Fortunately, the other teachers went easy on her because it was her first day. She never got called on. The other kids avoided her like the plague. Not that it mattered, Denise decided. As far as she could see, Ruthie would have gone on sketching if someone had driven a team of oxen right across her feet.

Finally, it was time for social studies. Denise marched along beside Ruthie silently, then nudged her into Room 112. Mrs Gaston wasn't there yet. She spent a great deal of time in the teachers' lounge. Denise guessed that she smoked. Before sitting down, Ruthie hesitated next to Mrs Gaston's desk. Twice she started to put the sketchbook on it. Twice she pulled it back. Finally, she dropped it on a pile of papers and sped away to her seat, clasping and twisting her hands nervously.

Denise watched her in fascination, her mind full to bursting with this mysterious new . . . friend? Hardly. Acquaintance? To be acquainted meant to *know* someone and Denise didn't feel she knew Ruthie *at all*. And yet, there she was, right beside her, just as she'd been all day. She was there and yet she wasn't there. A presence. That's what Ruthie was. A wispy presence, like a ghost. Or like the strange feeling Denise sometimes got on summer nights just before a thunderstorm broke.

"Well, what have we here?" Mrs Gaston asked, brightly. She'd sailed into the room and spotted Ruthie's sketchbook. As she thumbed through its pages, her eyes widened behind her bifocals and her mouth made a perfect little "o".

"Ruthie," she squealed, "did you do these?"

Ruthie gave that quick nod. Denise found she was getting

used to that nod. It was almost as if Ruthie had spoken a complete, civilised answer. "Yes, Mrs Gaston, I did those drawings of Boston. I did them in maths and I did them in English. I did them in the lunchroom, too." That's what that little bobbing head meant, all right.

"Why, these are simply marvellous! Class, look," Mrs Gaston announced, holding up one picture after another. "This is Boston Common. See? And Old North Church—you've heard me mention these things. And here's Milk Street. See the cobblestones? And there's the dock. Where the Boston Tea Party occurred, remember?"

"Yeeeeessssss."

The sound made Denise jump, not because it was so loud, but because it wasn't loud enough. There was Maxine, also glancing around the room in surprise. Only she and a few others had participated in that mocking outcry. Most of the class were admiring Ruthie's drawings. Denise felt herself swelling with pride, which made absolutely no sense, she knew. She had nothing at all to do with Ruthie's talent. But she *had* volunteered to help Ruthie when the others had refused. *Now* they were sorry, weren't they?

From the way Maxine whipped around in her seat and held her head high, Denise could tell she wasn't sorry, exactly; she was angry. Furious. People were finding some good in Ruthie when she, Maxine Fitzhugh the First, had decided already and for all time that Ruthie was not worth bothering with. Well!

Maxine was not the only one troubled by the art display and the reaction to it. Through it all, Ruthie kept her fists clenched in her lap, her eyes tightly closed and her head bowed. Glancing sideways at her several times, Denise felt embarrassed, as if she were intruding on something terribly private. She could see Ruthie's jaws working beneath the tight, pale skin of her cheek. She gnashed her teeth as each new picture was announced.

"Oh, Ruthie, these are simply marvellous," Mrs Gaston

crowed. "Thank you so much. May I hold onto them for a little while?"

Ruthie snapped erect. Her eyes flew open and she shook her head hard. It was more like a shudder. Mrs Gaston's smile fell to half-mast again and the sweetness in her voice took on a shrill edge.

"Well, we can certainly understand your not wanting anything to happen to them, Ruth. Thank you, just the same, for sharing them with us."

Stiffly, she minced down the aisle and placed the sketch-book on Ruthie's desk. Ruthie quickly shuffled it under her notebook. Mrs Gaston sighed, regarding the top of Ruthie's head pensively, as if trying to read her mind straight through her skull. Then, with a sudden burst of energy, she whirled and returned to the front of the room.

"Crazy as a loon," Denise heard Maxine mutter to Betsy.

Was she talking about Mrs Gaston? Or *Ruthie*? Probably Ruthie, Denise decided angrily. She resisted the urge to grab the bumpy closure of Maxine's bra and snap it so hard her ears would ring.

"All right, class, let's pass our current events assignments to the front of the room . . ."

Bucharest and its suffering thousands rode the sea of outstretched hands and landed on Mrs Gaston's desk along with all the other newspaper clippings and reports. For a moment, Denise suffered a twinge of guilt at abandoning the homeless, suffering thousands. But the earthquake was half a world away. And right beside her was this strange, sad, fascinating creature named Ruthie Morgenthau.

4

The house was empty when Ruthie arrived home from school. She placed her books on the desk in her bedroom and sat down on the bed.

It hadn't been as bad as she'd expected. But why, *why* had she drawn all those pictures like that? Like a *madwoman*. She'd been so nervous, so eager to please. At first, the drawing relaxed her. It helped her forget the new house, the new school, *everything*. Then she couldn't stop herself. And now, she didn't have the slightest idea of what had gone on in all those classes. How would she ever catch up? She *had* to do well in school. She couldn't let her mother down. Or Aunt Sarah. Especially not now. She was all they had left, really.

She'd ask Denise Riley to help her. Denise was okay. She was funny in some ways and kind of strong-willed, but kind, like Aunt Sarah. Except Denise was incredibly clumsy. She'd tripped over her own feet *three times* going down the hall. Once she almost knocked over a teacher. Then, while she was trying to apologise, she backed into the vice-principal, Mr Grinestaff.

She and Denise must've looked odd together, the long and the short of it. One big, soft, and awkward, the other little, bony, and timid.

Ruthie reached out for her sketchbook, then propped herself up on one elbow and opened it. She lingered briefly over the Boston pictures. Why hadn't she left them with Mrs Gaston? She recalled the cool glitter of the teacher's

34

eye, her plastic smile. Something about her frightened Ruthie, made her shiver in revulsion.

Quickly, she flipped to a fresh, clean page and reached for a sharp pencil. She'd begin with Denise's hair. It was clownlike, a wig of tight, red–gold curls. Ruthie smiled, remembering, as her pencil danced over the page, merrily scritch-scratching the minutes away.

The afternoon sun had long gone from the window and she was working almost in the dark when she heard her mother and Aunt Sarah coming in the back door. She smiled at the picture in her lap. She had caught Denise's awkwardness, elbows akimbo, one just about to collide with a locker door. And she'd caught the kindness in her face, too, the almost anxious caring, as if all the pain in the world were her personal responsibility.

"Ruthie? Where are you, *mamala*?" Aunt Sarah called.

"In here."

"Why are you working in the dark?"

Aunt Sarah flipped on the overhead light. It gave off a sickly yellow glow. "*Oi vey*, this could use another two hundred watts."

Undaunted, Aunt Sarah perched on the end of Ruthie's bed. Today she was wearing a green trouser suit with a man's shirt and tie. A diamond glittered from a tieclip at its centre. She looked very businesslike.

"So? How was school?"

"It was okay."

"Did you make some new friends."

"One, maybe. Denise Riley."

Aunt Sarah thought for a moment. "No, don't know her. And I thought I knew everybody in Deerfield. Working on the city council, I get complaints from everybody. She must come from a family of noncomplainers."

"I think so."

"Good. I like her already."

"Where's Mama?"

"In the kitchen. We did a little grocery shopping. She's unpacking."

"Oh. Okay."

"I take good care of her. Don't you worry."

"I'm not."

"And I am going to convince her to let you take bat mitzvah lessons. As far as Rabbi Davis is concerned, it's all arranged."

Suddenly, Ruthie felt faint. She brushed her hand across her forehead as if to wipe the dizziness away. Aunt Sarah was too wrapped up in what she was saying to notice.

"You're really going to enjoy it," she went on. "Rabbi Davis is an excellent teacher and a good man, through and through. When he came to Deerfield, to our little congregation of fifty families lost out here in the cornfields, I thought he was too good to stay. Surely, he'd move on to some big, important congregation in New York or Chicago. Boston, maybe. But he likes it here. And am I glad. He can't wait to meet you, *mamala*."

Ruthie avoided her aunt's eager smile.

"It all depends on Mama," she said, softly.

"In that case, it all depends on *me*. I'm not a politician for nothing, you know. A big deal on the city council. You know what they say there? Whatever Sarah wants, Sarah gets. How about that, huh? For a woman over sixty who's no spring chicken, that's really something, huh?"

"Yes, it is," Ruthie agreed.

"Of course, I don't always get what I want. But it *looks* that way, because when I lose, I'm a good loser." Aunt Sarah paused for breath, then continued in a quieter tone. "*Mamala*, do you remember the little things I used to teach you, you know, when your father wasn't looking? The blessings and things?"

"I remember."

Aunt Sarah cupped Ruthie's face in both her hands. "Good!" she said, happily. "You're a good girl, Ruthie."

36

"Thank you," Ruthie said, as best she could in Aunt Sarah's vicelike grip. Suddenly, Aunt Sarah let go of Ruthie and clapped her hands together.

"I bet I know a girl in your class," she said. "A Fitzhugh?"

"Yes. Maxine Fitzhugh."

"I thought so. Her father is not, how shall I say, my biggest fan."

"Why not?"

"Well, he's a developer. He builds and sells those little houses, maybe you've noticed them. They all look alike and they're so close together, you can see right into your neighbour's bathroom."

"Like this one?"

"Similar. But new. Well, if Mr Fitzhugh could have his way, he would build those falling-down cheap houses from one end of the city to the other. Just throw them up, get your money and let the suckers who buy do the best they can."

"Do they really fall down?"

"Well, I have no proof, but plenty of suspicions. And being on the city council, I have a little say in zoning and building permits and I've managed to stop Mr Fitzhugh from earning his second million dollars." Aunt Sarah winked one bright blue eye mischievously. "And the building code inspector is hot on his trail," she concluded, in a conspiratorial whisper.

Ruthie grinned. Somehow Aunt Sarah made an argument sound like an adventure.

Further gossip about Deerfield's prominent citizens kept the dinner conversation peppy, but when Aunt Sarah went home, she seemed to take all the energy and light out of the house with her. A gloom settled over everything. Ruthie and her mother got ready for bed in their separate rooms without a word to each other. At last, they muttered soft good nights and Ruthie kissed her mother's sallow cheek.

How can it be, she wondered, that Mama is almost fifteen years younger than Aunt Sarah, but she seems twenty years older?

It must have been just before dawn because the sky had a milky haze to it. Ruthie sat up in bed, confused, but only for a moment. Again the screams tore through the air; again and again they came, frightening and hurting her, leaving their invisible bruises everywhere. Ruthie clutched her head and tried to block them out.

"Nein! Nein!" her mother was shrieking. The screams rose to a wordless wail and then, after a very long time, sank into muffled sobbing. Ruthie huddled under her blanket and sobbed, too, as she had so many times before, grieving helplessly over her mother's pain, wishing, *praying* that she could end it, and then furious because she couldn't.

She knew better than to go to her mother and try to wake her up. She knew better than to ask what was wrong, what the nightmare was about. Her mother would deny everything, pretend nothing at all had happened. Or was she pretending? Did she even *know* she had nightmares?

The next morning was like a thousand other mornings. Mrs Morgenthau got breakfast quietly, efficiently, never referring to the night before or showing any sign that anything unusual had happened. Ruthie's Cheerios sat before her, almost untouched. Try as she might, she couldn't get a single spoonful past the lump in her throat.

"Eat, Ruth," her mother gently urged.

Ruthie looked up at the sweet, concerned face and lifted her spoon again, determined to please her mother in any way she could.

5

For the first time since starting Gardner Junior High, Denise
trotted towards school eagerly. On her way, she answered
the occasional "Hi" with an extra-cheerful "Good morning!" and ignored the surprised looks her classmates gave
each other afterwards. So she was weird. Let them live with
it. At least she was weird and happy!

She could hardly stay seated at her desk waiting for
Ruthie to arrive. Her blood seemed to be percolating cheeri-
ly in her veins: blubba-blubba-blipblip blub-blub-blup-
blipblip.

Suddenly, Betsy Williamson and a couple of other girls
scurried in, in high giggling form. Betsy was blushing huge
unsightly blotches all over her skinny face and neck.

"She did it! I never thought she'd really do it!" she was
squealing and spritzing.

A few seconds later, Maxine Fitzhugh swept in. Denise—
and everyone else—understood immediately why Betsy
was so red-faced. Maxine was sporting a brand-new T-
shirt, a masterpiece in black with dayglow letters. Much as
Denise hated to give her the satisfaction of reading today's
message, there was no way she could avoid it. "Let your
fingers do the walking," hot pink print shouted bumpily
across the front. Mountain-climbing, Denise thought.
Then Maxine swirled around to take her seat and the back of
the T-shirt presented her phone number, three inches tall
and shocking orange.

"Oh, no," Denise groaned. But no one heard her over the

whistles and hoots exploding all over the classroom. Heads, belonging in other classrooms, bobbed in and out of the doorway, eyes rolling, tongues flapping in the breeze. Maxine smiled innocently, radiant with self-satisfaction. She swivelled in her seat to talk to Betsy, a turn practically choreographed to show both sides of the message to any poor souls who might have missed them. Betsy's ordinarily adoring face looked as if all her blood had just clotted there and was never going to flow freely again.

Several of the boys made a big deal about copying down Maxine's phone number. A lot of good it would do them, Denise thought. Getting a date with Maxine was a lot like cashing a cheque: you had to show your driver's licence.

Suddenly, Mr Grinestaff, the vice-principal, appeared at the door.

"Maxine Fitzhugh," he snapped.

Maxine fluttered her hand above her head. "Here I am," she purred.

"I know where you are, young lady. Would you step into my office, please?"

There was total silence as Maxine pranced to the door.

Oh, good, Denise found herself hoping, let her get into trouble. Let her get suspended. I hope she's absolutely, totally, utterly and completely humiliated.

At the same time, Denise felt something like sympathy trickling along her spine. She hated to see anyone suffer. Even Maxine.

At the door, Maxine turned, treated the class to a big, sly wink, then disappeared. Everyone, except Denise, burst into applause. Maxine *humiliated*? Impossible! Even if she *did* get suspended, it wouldn't upset her. In fact, the rest of the class would probably try to get suspended too, just to be in fashion. Denise shoved a mental cork in her trickle of sympathy.

In the midst of the hubbub that followed Maxine's exit, Ruthie arrived. If the class had shown any interest in her the day before, it was forgotten now. Maxine was the Topic of the Day. She probably planned it that way, Denise mused. Ruthie could have painted an exact replica of the Sistine Chapel on the ceiling of the classroom and nobody would have noticed.

Except Denise. She noticed immediately that Ruthie was smiling at her as she approached her desk.

"Good morning, Ruthie," Denise sang out, beaming.

Ruthie bobbed her head. "Morning," she murmured shyly, busying herself with arranging her books into a perfectly aligned pile. "How are you?"

"I'm just great," Denise replied. "How about you?"

"I'm okay. Not so nervous as yesterday."

"Yeah, first days are rough. I know. I was the only girl from my sixth grade class assigned here."

"How come?"

"There's a new junior high on the southside. The cut-off line went right down the middle of my block. Did you like your old school in Boston?"

Ruthie shrugged. "It was all right."

"I loved Douglas Elementary. Green and white, the school colours, are still my favourite combination. I was president of the Women's Club."

"What's that?"

"Well, it was this club I thought up with a couple of my old friends. We were against the war in Vietnam, male chauvinist pigs, stuff like that. Men, you know, started all the world's problems and women are going to have to set them right. That's the truth, as far as I'm concerned. We had the club from fourth grade all the way through sixth. Almost every girl joined up. The boys hated it. Except secretly they were jealous."

"What did your club do?"

"We collected door-to-door for charities, we read everything we could about Gloria Steinem and Shirley Chisholm and Bella Abzug. Stuff like that."

"Do you still have the club?"

"No. We broke up when everybody except me went to Taft Junior High. At first we tried to keep on meeting, but it didn't work out. Everybody got kind of busy, I guess."

"Couldn't you start another club here?"

"With Maxine and the creeps from Thomas Elementary? Are you kidding? Nobody at Thomas ever thought about saving the world. Oh, no. The most they hoped for was permission to pierce their ears."

"Oh."

"They're *so* creepy. All they care about is dating and making out, although I bet Maxine is the only one who actually *does* it. For the first week or so, I pretended I was a captive queen in a hostile country, but that didn't help much. I used to speak out for human rights and stuff in social studies class, but I don't anymore. They just thought I was nuts."

"I don't think you're nuts," Ruthie said. "You remind me of my Aunt Sarah. She's always crusading for one cause or another."

"Oh, yeah?"

"Yeah. She's on the city council. Sarah Abrams."

"Oh. I haven't paid much attention to local politics. I've been too busy with national and international problems."

"Well, you'd like Aunt Sarah. She'd like you, too."

"Thanks. Hey, you know what? You look tired. Didn't you get enough sleep?"

At once, Ruthie's smile faded. Her eyelids fluttered and she began to fiddle nervously with her books again, lining them up with the biggest on the bottom and the smallest on top.

"I don't know," she mumbled. "Maybe not."

"Is something wrong?" Denise asked.

"No," Ruthie assured her. But Denise wasn't convinced. She eyed Ruthie's pale face curiously. What did she really know about this new girl? Nothing. She'd told Ruthie

42

almost all about her own past, but Ruthie hadn't volunteered a thing about herself. Just her Aunt Sarah. What was she hiding? Whatever it was, Denise sensed that it was something painful, not something bad she had done, but something she had suffered, maybe, something that had hurt her in a way she couldn't talk about.

The mystery of what that thing could be carried Denise through the rest of the day. As it turned out, Maxine did not get suspended. She just got a stern warning—which she related with great amusement in the gym locker room—and was sent home to change her shirt. She reappeared in the middle of music class and was greeted by a flurry of winks and victory signs. Her new shirt was more subdued. It had only a hand-painted heart on it, Denise observed, about where Maxine's heart—or a *normal* person's heart—was supposed to be. Some people have it all too easy, Denise concluded angrily, and others, like Ruthie, had it all too hard. Life was so *unfair!*

While the other girls chortled over Maxine's adventure, Denise slammed her gym locker so hard she caught her ring finger and practically ripped off the nail. Sucking her wound, she sailed past the cackling girls and out the door to catch up with Ruthie.

"Ruthie, wait!" she called across the gym. Her voice bounced off the shiny tiled walls of the huge empty room. "Can you come over to my house?"

"Now?"

"Uh-huh." The two girls fell into step, then stopped at Ruthie's locker.

"Well, I guess so. I'll have to call my mother."

"You can call from my house."

"Well, okay."

Just as Denise was wondering why Ruthie seemed so reluctant, Ruthie's face lit up with a new, pleased smile. Denise felt embarrassed at her own answering grin. She'd only asked Ruthie to come over. It wasn't *that* big a deal.

And yet, somehow it was. Somehow Ruthie made it seem terribly important.

Ruthie was so different from any girl Denise had ever known. She made Denise feel so many odd feelings, deep sadness one moment and glowing warmth the next. She was like a tiny magnifying glass, making everything near her bigger than life. She was a puzzle, too. And a magnet. Denise felt herself drawn to her as if by an unearthly force. But she didn't mind at all.

For the first time since midsummer—oh, ages and ages ago—she had a friend.

6

Denise's house was exactly what Ruthie had often dreamed a house should be, and everything that her own houses had never been. The house was a lot like Denise herself. It had bright, strong colours, orange yellow, and white, but it was a little funny and messy too. A forest of plants flourished in every possible corner and on every shelf, as if reaching out to embrace all the liveliness and warmth.

When Ruthie and Denise breezed in through the back door, they found Mr Riley scrubbing away at a huge pile of dishes that teetered dangerously all around the sink.

"Mom still at school?" Denise asked, pulling Ruthie through the kitchen like a tugboat. They dropped their books on the first uncluttered spot they could find, the living room sofa. As the books hit, a cloud of dust rose and glinted in the sunlight drifting through a picture window.

Denise faked a coughing fit and waved the dust away with both hands. "It's not always this bad," she croaked. "Sometimes it's worse."

Mr Riley's answer was shouted back above running water. "Mom won't be home till late. Big test coming up in Library Science 421. Aren't you going to introduce me?"

"Oh, sure." Denise swung around, appraising the room. "Oh, no," she sighed. Ruthie followed her glance and saw a clutter of coffee cups on various small tables, a laundry basket ready to burst its contents across the floor, an abandoned heap of not-quite-folded clothes on an easy chair and a card table at one wall piled with textbooks, magazines, a dress pattern, a stack of bills, a cheque book, an unfinished letter and one pencil, pocked with toothmarks and lacking a point.

"Give me a hand, okay?" Denise begged. Together they gathered the cups and toted them into the kitchen.

"Dad, this is Ruthie Morgenthau. She's just moved to Deerfield from Boston. This is my dad, Mr Riley."

"Hi, Ruthie," Mr Riley said, turning to face her. In a flash, his smile collapsed and he groaned, "Oh, no, not *more*. Do those cups belong to us or are the neighbours bringing me their dirty dishes, too?"

"Our very own," Denise assured him.

"Don't you think we ought to use paper plates and cups?"

"No," Denise answered firmly. "They are ecologically wasteful."

Mr Riley moaned mournfully and renewed his attack on the dishes. "I suppose you're right," he grumbled, "but you'll be sorry tomorrow when it's your turn." He winked at Ruthie conspiratorially and she giggled.

Denise pulled a dish towel off the rack and tossed it to Ruthie. "You dry, I'll put away," she announced and began tossing a jumble of cutlery into a drawer. "How come you're home so early?" she asked her father.

"Well, I got that grant proposal mailed off today and felt great for about two hours. Then I made the big mistake of eating lunch. One hot pastrami on rye and I couldn't keep my eyes open. Then I remembered I hadn't been to bed last night. So I came home and treated myself to a nap. I just got up about half an hour ago."

"You mean you worked all night? You didn't get to bed at all?"

"That's right."

"Wow! What's it like to stay up all night? I'd like to do that sometime."

"Terrific. I'll let you write the next proposal."

"Really?"

"No. Riley."

"Ho, ho, ho." Denise slammed the drawer shut and jerked open a cabinet. "Well, I hope you get your grant," she said, piling plates onto the shelf.

"Thanks, Pumpkin. Me, too. I'd miss those pastramis on rye."

"Would we really be that hard up for money if you didn't get the grant?"

"Well, kiddo, your mom's got at least two more years to go on her Ph.D. Once she gets it and goes to work, we'll be fine. But until then . . ."

Ruthie listened silently as Denise and Mr Riley bantered back and forth and teased each other. She sighed contentedly and polished each dish and cup until it glowed. Inside, her every nerve ending was atingle as she pulled in the atmosphere of the Riley house and of Denise and her father, so at ease with each other as they worked side by side. It was really incredible.

"My mom's going to be a medical librarian," Denise informed Ruthie, proudly. Ruthie nodded, not at all sure what a medical librarian was. She couldn't imagine anyone as energetic and boisterous as Denise locked away in a library all day. But maybe Mrs Riley was different. What *would* she be like? She'd be nice, that was certain. Only *good* things seemed possible in this house.

Finished with the dishes at last, Mr Riley flicked water off his fingertips, showering Denise and Ruthie, who blinked and gasped in surprise.

"Daddy!" Denise yelped. She lunged for the sprinkler hose on the sink, but her father caught her by the wrist.

"No, no," he pleaded. "You'll make a mess."

"Oh, okay," Denise said, relenting. She laughed and gave her father a loud and sloppy kiss on the cheek.

Watching them, Ruthie felt suddenly overwhelmed with longing. So this is how it really is for other families, she thought. Like a TV show. Like a fairy tale. Or a dream.

47

"Can Ruthie stay for dinner?" Denise asked her father.

"Oh, no," Ruthie said quickly. "No, I couldn't. And I'd better call my mother right away. I completely forgot."

"What's the matter?" Mr Riley wondered, his eyes twinkling. "Don't you like canned ravioli? It's my speciality."

Ruthie blushed. "No, it's not that. I . . ."

Suddenly, she felt Mr Riley's broad hand gently ruffling her hair. Her whole body shivered in a crazy mixture of shock and pleasure.

"Never mind," he was saying. "The phone's right over there on the wall. Or there's one upstairs, if you'd rather."

"Thank you," Ruthie replied, fascinated by the open friendliness on Mr Riley's thin, lightly freckled face. She had very little experience of fathers other than her own, but she often dreamed of one exactly like this. There was no anger in his eyes, no sorrow furrowing his brow and drawing his lips in a straight line. He was happy in a way Ruthie had always wished people could be happy. She'd wondered if somewhere somebody's father was like this, relaxed and cheerful, but she'd always doubted it because of the only family she knew well, her own.

"I like your father," Ruthie told Denise when they were settled upstairs in Denise's bedroom with a bag of chocolate chip cookies and two mugs of milk.

"He's a good guy," Denise agreed. "He's smart, too. He's a physiologist. He does research."

"On diseases?"

"Pure research," Denise explained. "That means they just explore things without knowing what they might find. It could be a cure for a disease. They never know." She popped off a chocolate chip and chewed it thoughtfully. "These are a little stale," she said, grimacing. "I'm sorry."

"They're okay," Ruthie replied.

"What does your father do?"

"He's dead." The words surprised Ruthie as she said them. They sounded so strange, so unreal. When had she last talked about her father's death with anyone? She couldn't remember.

"Oh, I'm sorry."

Ruthie shrugged. "He was a tailor. He and my mother had a little shop in Boston. In the old country, they worked for a big company."

"The old country?"

"Germany. They came here from Germany. In 1948."

"Really? That's very interesting. Mine came from Nebraska. It's not too interesting, but it's fun. We go there a lot. Have you ever been to Germany?"

"No." Ruthie took a sip of milk and found it hard to swallow. She didn't like the questions she knew were coming. Her insides quaked at the thought. So many questions. And so many she had no answers for. And so many she could not bear to answer. Part of her wanted to run away, to put down the milk and the cookie and leave, quickly, before it was too late. But part of her longed for Denise's friendship. There had never been anyone quite like her in Boston, so full of life and so caring, so gentle. You just knew she would never, ever hurt you, no matter what. Ruthie took another sip of milk, and stayed.

"Do you still have relatives in Germany?" Denise was wondering.

"No," Ruthie replied, wishing it were over, desperate for a way to skip over this part. "There's no one left."

"Oh. Mine all still live in Nebraska. Just outside of Lincoln. All four of my grandparents and . . . let's see . . . three uncles, three aunts and . . . um . . . seven, no *eight* cousins. Aunt Louise just had another one. Her fourth, isn't that something? We visit them almost every summer. When we get together it's like a circus. Once I laughed and yelled so much, I had laryngitis for two weeks afterwards. And I have one cousin, Danny, who looks a lot like Todd

49

Jones, only he's older and nicer. Are your grandparents still in Boston?"

"I don't have any grandparents," Ruthie managed to say. "My mother and my Aunt Sarah are the only relatives I know. Aunt Sarah has children—even grandchildren—but they all live on the West Coast. I've never met them."

Denise's mouth fell open. "I've never heard of such a small family. Just a mother and an aunt. Wow."

Ruthie watched Denise's face fill with sadness, with pity for *her*. She couldn't stand that, and had to stop it somehow. Quickly, she set her milk on the night table and jumped to her feet. "Do you know what I'd like?" she said.

"What?"

"I'd like to pretend that I'm your sister and that I live in this house and have all your relatives."

She danced around the room while Denise laughed and said, "That's fine with me. I hate being an only child. Don't you?"

Ruthie stopped in mid-twirl, her back to Denise. "Yes," she said, her voice rasping painfully in her throat. "Yes, I hate being an only child."

"Well, we're not anymore. Now we're sisters, okay? Let's shake on it."

Ruthie turned and took Denise's outstretched hand. It was warm and soft next to her own slender, cool fingers.

"Okay," she agreed. For the rest of the afternoon, she refused to think about anything sad. She willed herself to giggle and chat and pretend as hard as she could that she really belonged in Denise's household.

Returning home that evening was almost more than Ruthie could bear. It was twilight when she stepped into the living room. The heavy curtains were closed, just as they had been when she left for school that morning. In fact, the whole house was dark. It could just as well have been midnight. Her mother must have gone out with Aunt Sarah. But why were all the blinds and curtains still drawn? Had she sat there all day, in the dark, until Aunt Sarah came? Ruthie knew that was very likely. Suddenly, she found herself shaking with rage. Why did it have to be like this? Why couldn't she have a happy house to come home to like Denise? Why did she have to go on suffering for something that happened long before she was born? It wasn't fair!

She ran into her mother's room and yanked open the middle dresser drawer. It was a different dresser from the old apartment. Its blondness looked plastic compared to the heavy walnut furniture they'd left behind. But the contents of the middle drawer were exactly the same. There were a few handkerchiefs, worn but neatly folded to show her mother's delicate embroidery around their edges, a green velvet box with a rusty hinged lid, and, pushed towards the back, a beige flat box that had once probably contained a tie. Now, and as far back as Ruthie could remember, it held a mass of photographs. Ruthie lifted an edge of the box; yes, they were still there. She felt a lump swelling in her throat and tears burning her eyes. She would not look at them again. Never, never again.

But her trembling hand, acting with a will of its own, reached out for the little ring box. Sobbing, Ruthie snapped it open. Its hinges squeaked in protest and the locket inside fell into the drawer. Ruthie retrieved it and peered at the tiny picture through the blur of her tears.

"Sister," she whispered, and sank to her knees on the floor. Clutching the locket and crying, she rocked back and forth. "Sister," she echoed, "Sister." The word ached as she wrenched it out.

Suddenly, she sat upright and listened. Yes, her mother was returning. In no time, the locket was back in her drawer, the drawer was quietly shut and Ruthie was in the bathroom, slapping cold water against her ashen cheeks and swollen eyes.

7

Denise read over her notes and began to giggle.

"I wrote down Nov Nov," she told Ruthie.

But Ruthie was busy sketching, the pad held up almost to her nose so that Denise couldn't see what was on it. "What?" she asked, without much interest.

"I accidently wrote down Nov Nov," Denise repeated. "For the history report. What did Gaston say, November fifth or sixth? God, she talks so fast sometimes, I think my arm's going to fall off before I get it all down." Denise inked out the second Nov, making a careful little box like a coffin and then colouring it in. "So what was it, the fifth?"

Ruthie went on working. "I don't know. I thought you had it, so I didn't write it down."

"Oh, terrific," Denise sighed. "Well, let's see if we can catch somebody and ask before they're all gone."

"Okay. In a minute," Ruthie mumbled, obviously not about to budge in the next sixty seconds.

"What are you working on there?"

"Mrs Gaston," Ruthie announced, sounding very pleased with herself. She tilted her head, appraising the picture, then made a few more hasty pencil strokes. Finally, she turned the sketchbook around and held it up for Denise to see.

"Oh, will you look at that!" Denise crowed.

Todd Jones happened to be passing the abandoned history room just in time to hear her.

"What's she got?" he wanted to know. "More Boston?"

He sauntered in, soon followed by Elizabeth Harrison, who worshipped him even though she was a year older, and a gaggle of her girl friends.

"Hey!" Todd exclaimed. "Gaston the goat! Hey, Parker," he shouted over his shoulder, "come here a second. Look at this."

In no time at all, a small mob had gathered around Ruthie, Denise, and the picture, oohing, aahing, and guffawing over Gaston the goat: Mrs Gaston's quite recognisable head rising from the elongated neck and body of a nanny goat. Out from between her nastily smiling thin lips protruded the remnants of a well-gnawed social studies textbook.

Denise beamed proudly at Ruthie, who was taking the jokes and compliments with only minor hand twitching and eyelid fluttering. She appeared genuinely pleased.

But wherever a crowd gathered, Maxine Fitzhugh was bound to appear, much like the unwanted thirteenth fairy.

"What's all the fuss?" she demanded to know. Like the waters of the Red Sea, the crowd parted to let her through. Everyone grew quiet, waiting for her ultimate judgment. Maxine paused a hushed moment for full effect.

"How cute," she chirped. Then, apparently realising she was very close to the centre of attention, she spun around and announced: "Guess what, everybody?"

"What?" Betsy Williamson piped up from the back of the crowd. She jumped up and down and waved to show Maxine where her ever-faithful support was coming from.

"I think I'm going to be nominated for Sigma Iota Princess."

"That's impossible," Elizabeth Harrison protested. "You have to be in high school."

Maxine sashayed back up the aisle, the seat of her super-tight jeans bouncing rhythmically. "In my case," she sang, "they *may* make an exception. We were all hanging out at

53

HoJo's last night and that's exactly what they said: an exception."

Some people shrugged and scrunched up their mouths in disbelief. Others exchanged impressed glances. But they all followed Maxine out the door, as if Ruthie and Gaston the goat had never existed.

"Oh, well," Denise said, "Let's go to the library. You want to? We can get a headstart on our reports. Oh, I forgot to ask if they're due the fifth or the sixth. Nuts."

"Doesn't matter," Ruthie said, folding up her sketch-book and tucking it under her others. She dropped her pencil into her bulging denim totebag and stood up.

"You know what my father and mother say about Maxine's father?" Denise offered as the two crossed the Public Square on their way to the library.

"What?"

"They say he and your Aunt Sarah are going to have a big showdown one of these days."

"What do you mean?"

"Well, there's some property he wants to buy from the city and she's against it."

"She's against everything he does, I guess. She says he builds junky houses."

"Yeah. Well, she was on the news last night."

"I know, at the council meeting."

"I caught just a glimpse of her. She's so *little*."

"Yeah. But tough."

"She's really cute. I loved it when she waggled her finger right under the reporter's nose and told him, 'I'm three times your age and so I'm three times smarter, no?' She wasn't the least bit shy about it."

"Oh, no, not Aunt Sarah. She's used to getting her own way."

"Well, my mom and dad said she's going to have a big fight this time. I guess old Fitzhugh's used to getting his way, too. Rich people are spoiled rotten, I think."

54

"Well, I don't think Aunt Sarah's spoiled, exactly. She wasn't always rich. Uncle Izzy left her a lot when he died. Between the insurance and selling the jewellery business . . . yeah, she's rich, now."

"We'll never be rich," Denise mused. "Are you rich?"

Ruthie laughed. "No. Aunt Sarah would buy us everything we needed if my mother'd let her, but she won't."

"Why not? I'd let her."

"I don't know. Aunt Sarah wants me to have a bat mitzvah. She wants to pay for everything."

"What's a bat mitzvah?"

"Oh, I keep forgetting you're not Jewish."

"I don't even *know* anyone Jewish, except you."

"Well, where we lived in Boston, everybody was Jewish. Here, Aunt Sarah says there are only fifty Jewish families."

"So what's a bat mitzvah?"

"It means Daughter of the Law. It's a ceremony when a girl turns thirteen. For boys, it's called *bar* mitzvah, Son of the Law. It means you're an adult in the eyes of the congregation and you have to take responsibility for yourself. For being a good Jew, which mainly means following the Ten Commandments. That's what it means by the Law."

"What do you have to do?"

"Actually, I'm not sure. I have to read a passage from the Torah, I know that."

"The Torah?"

"The first five books of Moses. From the Old Testament, you know?"

"Oh, sure."

"Well, the first five books are on these scrolls and I'd have to read part of it in front of everybody. In Hebrew."

"Can you read Hebrew?"

"No. I'd have to go to Rabbi Davis for lessons. And there are a bunch of blessings to learn, too, I think."

"Haven't you ever been to a bat . . . a whatchamacallit?"

"Bat mitzvah. Once, with my aunt. But it was a long time ago."

"How come only once?"

A red light stopped the two girls at a street corner. Denise looked at Ruthie and saw that she was watching the passing cars as if she hadn't heard the question.

"How come you've only seen one bat mitzvah? I mean, if everybody was Jewish."

The light turned green and Ruthie stepped off the curb. It wasn't until they'd hurried across the street that she answered.

"We never went to synagogue. My father was against it."

"Against organised religion? My parents are like that. But we're Unitarians because they hang pretty loose."

"No, he was against Judaism."

"But you're Jewish! That doesn't make any sense."

"I know. But that's the way he was. Anyway, when I'm thirteen, in June, I have to make my own decisions about religion. That's the whole point."

"So are you going to do it, the . . . um . . . the mitzvah thing?"

"Bat mitzvah. I don't know. Aunt Sarah really wants me to. A lot. She wants to have a dinner dance afterwards and everything. The biggest party you've ever seen, she says. I don't know why she wants to make such a big deal out of it. It's not as if we have a huge family to invite, or even a lot of friends."

Suddenly, Ruthie raced ahead, taking the library steps two at a time. While a surprised Denise lumbered after her, she tossed her books onto the first table she came to, then hurried off to a row of shelves, examining it intensely as if searching for an enormously important book.

Denise piled her own books next to Ruthie's. What had gone wrong? What had upset Ruthie like that? Was it not having a father and grandparents and aunts and uncles and cousins? Denise sighed, supposing that was it. She knew she couldn't imagine life without the Nebraska crowd. Poor Ruthie! So alone in the world. Denise wished she could really share her whole family with Ruthie somehow.

She followed Ruthie around one bend and down the next aisle, unsure of what might happen next. The books in this area were on flowers and gardening, she noticed. What was Ruthie looking for here?

"Ruthie?" she called softly.

Ruthie was slumped against a shelf, her back to Denise.

"What?"

"Our reports are supposed to be on state history. Indians and settlers and stuff. That's all upstairs."

"You go ahead," came the reply. "I'll catch up with you."

"Are you okay?"

"Yeah, I'm all right. You go on."

"Well, okay." Denise waited a moment to make extra sure, but Ruthie remained as she was, leaning against the shelf, her head bowed, her arms crossed in front of her as if she were hugging herself against the cold. Only it wasn't cold. The library was overheated; its high narrow windows steamed over. Finally, Denise turned away and went upstairs.

She decided she'd do her report on a local Indian tribe. They sounded more interesting than the settlers. She ran a finger along the dingy rows of books on the Plains Indians until she came to what had to be the newest book. It had a protective plastic cover and a full-colour illustration on the front. There were lots of paintings and photographs inside and the print was just right: not too big, like a kid's book, and not too small and footnoted like the dull stuff her mother groaned over every night as she underlined fact after boring fact. Denise sat down at the nearest study table and began to read.

The next thing she knew, she was almost through chapter three and Ruthie still hadn't come upstairs. Tucking the book under her arm, she walked quickly from one aisle to the next, checking up and down and around the other study tables. No Ruthie.

Denise took the stairs down, constantly checking behind her in case Ruthie got off the elevator. But she didn't. From halfway down the stairs, Denise thought she caught a glimpse of Ruthie's blue-striped blouse sticking out from behind a shelf at the back of the room. She hurried towards the spot, but when she got there, Ruthie was gone. Denise peered around to the next aisle. There she was, her back towards Denise, two books under her arm, the third in her hands. She was frantically flipping pages, unaware of Denise's presense. Denise was just about to ask what was going on when Ruthie did an extremely odd thing. She slipped all three books into her totebag and zipped it closed!

Immediately, Denise ducked back where Ruthie wouldn't see her. Her heart was slamming against her chest. What in the world was Ruthie doing? Why would she steal books from the library? It was crazy. And besides, Ruthie was *honest*, ridiculously honest. Once, when Denise's mother had said they could have a "couple of cookies," Denise had to *convince* Ruthie it was all right to take *three*!

Denise silently slipped back to the check-out desk. The librarian had already stamped her Plains Indians book when Ruthie finally appeared at her side.

"Ready to go?" she asked. Her face was ghostly pale and she was blinking nervously.

"Yes," Denise said, trying to sound normal. "Did you find a book?"

"What? Oh, no, nothing I liked."

"Well, there's still time. You can look some more if you want."

"No, that's okay. Another day, maybe."

Together they descended the library steps. Denise felt so tense she could hardly move her feet. She couldn't have felt more guilty if she'd actually taken those books herself. For the first half mile, while their routes home coincided, she didn't dare look at Ruthie and neither of them spoke a word. Denise listened to the scuffling of their shoes, the whoosh of rush-hour traffic, the barking of a faraway dog. There was so much she wanted to say.

When they got to the corner where they had to separate, Denise finally managed a hushed, "See you tomorrow." Ruthie just nodded and walked away, her brows furrowed as if she were deep in some troubling thought. For a moment, Denise watched her friend wander off into her own dream world. Or was it a nightmare world? Denise wondered.

8

In spite of everything, sketching still worked. Long ago, Ruthie had discovered that the more she sketched, the less things bothered her. And tonight, while her hand flew over the pages, nothing bothered her at all. Not the library books hidden at the back of her closet, not even the voices of her mother and aunt filtering through her closed door from the kitchen. The voices rose and fell in disagreement. Ruthie could hear only parts of what they were saying, the louder parts, which were mostly Aunt Sarah's. Ordinarily, it would have upset her a lot, as many arguments and whispered conversations had in the past when Aunt Sarah, and sometimes Uncle Izzy, had visited them in Boston. Countless nights had passed in trembling agony, huddled under her blanket, crying alone, when the adults thought she was long asleep. But now, she found that the time she passed sketching was peaceful, no matter what was going on around her.

She filled pages with portraits of people at school. Todd Jones and Billy Parker turned up pictured as a pair of clowns. Billy was fat and grinning; Todd, thin and serious and undeniably handsome even in the polka-dotted clown suit. Ruthie suspected that Denise liked Todd. Even though she called him a male chauvinist pig, she spent an awful lot of time noticing where he was and what he was doing.

"Hannah, listen to me. If it weren't for him . . ."

Another picture was of Mr Babcock, their meek and meticulous science teacher. His high-pitched voice was mimicked by almost everyone at least once a day and was always good for a laugh. Ruthie drew him as a canary, daintily perched in an ornately curlicued cage. His bright, beady eyes fitted the image perfectly.

"What's gone is gone, Hannah. You must stop living in the . . ."

Mr Grinestaff, whose every gruff speech before an assembly ended with "You play fair with me and I'll play fair with you," donned a pirate's uniform and set forth, steel-jawed, to sail a tempestuous sea at the helm of a bloody pirate ship.

"Let me talk to her, all right? You don't even . . ."

Ruthie put down her pencil and slowly let the sketchbook slide off her lap onto the rumpled white bedspread. Anxiety tingled in her veins as Aunt Sarah's high-heeled boots clopped towards her door. The brand-new boots, worn with dresses and slacks alike, were meant to give the illusion of height. Instead, Aunt Sarah appeared to be two-thirds body and one-third foot. Ruthie considered sketching her as a silver-haired Minnie Mouse.

"Ruthie? Sweetheart? You're not asleep with the light on, are you?"

"No, Aunt Sarah. I'm awake."

The door creaked open and Aunt Sarah stood framed in the doorway, warm and cuddly in her beige bulky sweater and slacks, and smiling cheerfully as if nothing more emotionally charged than the weather had been discussed in the last hour and a half.

"Come into the kitchen, *mamala*. Your mother and I want to talk to you."

Ruthie swung her legs over the side of the bed and slipped her feet into her bedroom slippers. She shuffled after her aunt like a convict being marched to the electric chair.

Under the yellow kitchen light, her mother looked awful. Her face was gaunt and her shoulders slumped as though she were exhausted after some great physical effort.

61

Ruthie sank into a kitchen chair, waiting, like a convict, for a verdict of guilty, an unappealable sentence of death by slow torture. What was she guilty of? She wasn't sure. But whenever her mother looked like this, Ruthie felt it must somehow be her fault.

Aunt Sarah, blissfully ignorant of all this, began talking: "Your mother and I agree that the bat mitzvah decision should be left up to you."

Ruthie looked from her aunt to her mother, searching for a hint, a sign, of what she should do. Her mother's face was blank. She seemed to cringe slightly, as if expecting a blow.

"Mama? What do *you* want me to do?"

"Look," Aunt Sarah intervened, "she's already agreed it's up to you. What do *you* want to do, Ruthie?"

"I want to do whatever she wants me to do."

Aunt Sarah sighed. "*Mamala*, listen to me," she said, leaning across the table and tapping one silver nail in front of Ruthie to emphasise her words, "the only reason not to have a bat mitzvah is because your father, in his last years, was against everything to do with his religion. It was a madness with him. A vengeance against everything he'd been through."

"Sarah, please," Mrs Morgenthau begged. She propped one elbow on the table and covered her mouth with her hand as if to hold back her emotions.

Aunt Sarah held up her hand as if stopping traffic. "All right, all right, we don't have to go into it. But it *was* crazy. He wanted to wipe out his heritage, forget it, bury it. Well, you should pardon my bluntness—although, I, too, have lost a husband—he is gone and buried now, may he rest in more peace than he ever knew here, which, God knows, was too little. From Germany, though, to the end of his life, *he had his way*, which in my eyes and your Uncle Izzy's eyes, was wrong, although we understood even as we disapproved. But it's your life, now, Ruthie. And you should begin to live it. Not *his* way, *your* way."

On the verge of tears, Ruthie turned back to her mother. "Mama?" she pleaded.

Mrs Morgenthau shook her head, unable to reply.

"Mama, you've got to answer me. In *your* eyes, was Papa wrong?"

The delicately lined, shaking hand with its faint brown age spots moved to cover Mrs Morgenthau's eyes.

Suddenly, Aunt Sarah grabbed her by the shoulders.

"Don't!" Ruthie cried, scraping back her chair as she lunged towards her aunt.

But Aunt Sarah's grasp was as gentle as it was firm. "Tell her, Hannah," she urged, "tell her what you told me. She's incredible, your mother, Ruthie. She has spent so much time not wanting anything for herself, *afraid* to want anything for herself, she's forgotten how. But she said—and I swear this on my Izzy's grave—she told me if, God willing, she could have it all to do over again, without the pain and the suffering and the fear, you would be bat mitzvahed."

"Is that true, Mama?"

Slowly, Mrs Morgenthau looked up, not directly at Ruthie, but past her, through her, as if looking back through a warp in time to another life in another world. Her almost colourless grey eyes glistened at whatever it was she saw there and she nodded her head. A faint smile played on her lips, which she quickly bit to keep from trembling.

"You would be glad if I did it?" Ruthie asked.

Another nod.

Ruthie paused and watched her mother carefully. Where was she and who was she talking to? Not here, not me, she thought.

"If Mama wants it, I'll do it," she announced quietly.

Immediately, Aunt Sarah leaped to her feet with an exhilarated shriek. Tears and her howls of "Thank God!" mingled in a tangle of hugs and kisses that smelled faintly of garlic and a heady French perfume. Ruthie was almost

63

smothered in her delighted aunt's bosom, and actually gasped for air when she was finally let go.

"What an affair this will be," Aunt Sarah cooed. "Everyone in Deerfield is hereby invited, the Jews and Gentiles alike. And half of Boston, too. Why not? We'll have dinner, dancing. The whole congregation will be there, of course. Ruthie, sweetheart, you invite your whole class, the treat's on me."

Now Aunt Sarah was doing a makeshift *hora* around the kitchen table. *"Hoi, hoi, hoi, hoi, hoi, hoi,"* she sang, clapping out the rhythm with her hands, the diamond rings flashing above her head.

Mrs Morgenthau shook her head in disbelief. Ruthie laughed. But deep down, she was troubled. Why did everyone in Deerfield have to come to her bat mitzvah? She knew people had huge parties to celebrate, but why should she? Usually there were big family gatherings, but this was all the family she had. Heaven knew, she and her mother didn't need all that extravagance. For whom was Aunt Sarah doing it? She waited until Aunt Sarah had danced herself out and was once again seated at the table, one bejewelled hand to her bosom, gleefully huffing and puffing.

"Aunt Sarah, why does it have to be such a big bat mitzvah? I don't want my whole class there. Maybe just Denise and her family."

"Whoever you want," Aunt Sarah gasped. Not really responding to Ruthie, she raved on, "This is our moment of triumph. In spite of everything, another generation will read from the Torah, another generation of *our* family, *your* family, Hannah, believe it or not. We're alive! *L'chaim! L'chaim!* To life! It's a miracle, huh, Hannah? It's a miracle, no?"

But Mrs Morgenthau had slipped into another of her reveries, her hands quietly folded on her lap, her thoughts far away. This was another kind of miracle, one with which

Rutie was more familiar, the miracle that took her mother away. To what? To where? And most important, to whom? And why did she always seem happier there?

Late that night, Ruthie lay in bed thinking about Aunt Sarah and the bat mitzvah. Maybe Aunt Sarah was right. This was a new place, with a new home and a new friend. Maybe she, too, should stop living in the past and start all over, brand-new, fresh and clean. It seemed like a wonderful idea and if Aunt Sarah could do it, why couldn't she? She *could*. At least, she had to try.

But even as she promised herself a new start, Ruthie could see, through her tightly closed eyelids, glowing with a ghostly light, the books in her closet, the photographs in her mother's drawer and the sweet, sad face in her mother's locket.

9

Denise watched Ruthie until she was out of sight. The bouncing totebag slung over her shoulder was the last thing to disappear around the corner. Then Denise began to run towards home. She didn't want to think about Ruthie stealing books, she really didn't. She tried to focus her entire attention on the pounding of her sneakers against the pavement. She ran clutching her books against her ribs until her arms and legs ached. When her throat felt seared from the breath tearing through it, she was glad. It gave her something else to think about. When a cramp stabbed at her side, she was glad of that, too. She shifted her books to press against the pain and kept running. When sweat began to burn her eyes, she welcomed it. Anything, anything to shut out the image of Ruthie dropping those books into her totebag. Why? Why had she done it?

Finally, Denise had to slow down, and at that instant, she tripped over a crack in the broken pavement and went sprawling, her books skidding ahead of her. A huge slab was ripped off the left knee of her jeans and a smaller slab was scraped off her knee as well. As she sat there, pressing her aching knee and gasping for breath, she heard two boys' voices behind her. Too exhausted to turn around, she just prayed silently that the boys were not from Gardner Junior High.

"I'm telling," the older voice was saying.

"You better not," the younger one squeaked. "You better not tell. Please, Joey, don't tell. I tried to go, but somebody was in there. They wouldn't let me in. It'll dry. Look, it's almost dry."

"Mom'll know anyway."

"No, she won't. Not if you don't tell. Come on, Joe, don't tell."

The conversation stopped when the boys reached Denise. Joey put a protective arm on the younger boy's shoulder to steer him clear of Denise and the broken pavement. They skirted Denise with quick, curious glances, observing the scattered books but not touching them. Satisfied that Denise was neither dangerous nor a friend, Joey released his brother and renewed his teasing.

"Mom always knows stuff like that. You can't hide it. So I might as well tell her and get it over with."

He started to run now, loping ahead at an easy pace for his own long legs, but causing the little one to waddle frantically to keep up, obviously uncomfortable in his wet pants. Denise's heart went out to him. Joey was a total creep, no doubt about it. She hoped he'd wet his own pants some day, preferably while giving an oral book report. How could a kid be so cruel to his own little brother? Nothing made sense anymore, people least of all.

Denise inspected her knee. The bleeding had stopped. She pulled herself to her feet, gathered her books, and limped home.

"Pumpkin?" her mother called from somewhere upstairs. "Is that you?"

"Yes, it's me. I'm home."

Denise hesitated at the foot of the stairs. How to get to her room without passing her mother on the way? She wasn't ready to face her parents just yet. She wanted to be alone to think about Ruthie. She'd already decided not to tell her parents or anyone else about the books. She was no Joey the rat, that was for sure. Whatever Ruthie's problem was, Denise was her best friend and would protect her, no matter what.

Mrs Riley padded barefoot down the stairs.

"What happened to your jeans?" she cried in dismay.

"I tripped on the way home from the library."

"Not again! I swear you are harder on your clothes than a two-year-old child." Mrs Riley stooped over and jabbed a finger into the gaping hole.

"Watch my knee!" Denise yelped.

"Oh, you'll heal," Mrs Riley assured her. "But your jeans will need major surgery. Have you been practising ballet?"

"Well, not really."

"Well, *really*, you'd better. Go upstairs and clean up your wound there. Use antiseptic. Then change your clothes and you can practise for half an hour before dinner."

Denise groaned, but her mother was already on her way to the kitchen and missed the dramatic effect. If there was anything in the world Denise did not want to do just then, it was practise ballet. Who in the world could *dance* after what she'd just been through? She trailed after her mother and watched her open a tin of peas and dump them into a noodle casserole.

"What are you standing there for?" Mrs Riley wondered. "Is your knee that bad?"

Denise shook her head, fished a lump of tuna out of the casserole and munched on it.

"Then please go and change your jeans. And try not to eat dinner before I've cooked it."

"Okay," Denise said, eyeing another tempting morsel of tuna, but deciding against it. "Mom?"

"What?"

"When you were a kid, did you ever steal anything?"

Mrs Riley put down the empty can slowly, then turned to face Denise. "Are you in some kind of trouble?" she asked.

"No. I was . . . just wondering."

"How did you tear your jeans?"

"I told you. I tripped and fell on my way home from the library. You know me, I fall all the time, winter, spring, and summer, too."

68

"Very funny, very funny. Why do you want to know if I ever stole anything?"

"I was just curious. Ah . . . one of my classmates may have and I was wondering . . . why someone would do something like that. I've never done it."

Mrs Riley leaned one hip against the counter and grinned. "No, I don't think you ever have. Well, I'll tell you, I stole a ball-point pen once, from a classmate in third grade. The teacher had told us a dozen times to remember to bring a ball-point pen. We were beginning to write longhand, you know, cursive, as you call it now. And I forgot. I couldn't admit I'd forgotten. It would have been so humiliating if the teacher got angry at me—I was her pet, after all, and had a reputation to keep up. Anyway, there was Annie Wanamaker's pen, just sitting there on the desk next to mine. So I took it."

"What did Annie Wanamaker do?"

"She went home sick. Everything made poor Annie go home sick. Poor kid, she was a nervous wreck. I'll never forget it. I feel guilty about it to this day and I guess I always will."

Denise smiled. She loved to hear stories about when her mother was a little girl. She sensed, though, that this one was supposed to make it easier for Denise to talk about what was bothering her. Her mother did stuff like that all the time. But in this case, it wasn't enough. Stealing a kid's pen was a far cry from stealing books from the library. On the other hand, this Annie Wanamaker was intriguing. Was she like Ruthie?

"What makes a kid nervous like that? Like Annie Wanamaker?"

"Oh, wow, I don't know. In Annie's case, I think it was her mother. She was a nervous wreck, too. For the first three weeks of kindergarten, she stood outside our classroom door, afraid to leave Annie alone. Finally, *that* made Annie go home sick, so she stopped it. Poor old Annie. She

69

moved away after third grade and I never got a chance to apologise, let alone return the pen."

Mrs Riley gazed out the window dreamily for a moment, then snatched up a spoon and began stirring the casserole.

"Now, listen," she told Denise, "if you're sure you're not in trouble and/or pain, will you please go and do what you're supposed to do—or you *will* be in trouble and/or pain." She tweaked Denise's nose. Her hand gave off a delicious oniony smell. Laughing, Denise tried to break away, but her bad knee brought her up short.

"I can't dance," she moaned. "I'm lame. I'm a broken person."

As Mrs Riley raised one eyebrow in disbelief, Denise limped away and dragged her battered limb up the stairs.

Gingerly, she removed her torn jeans and propped her sore leg on the bathtub rim. Flinching as the soapy water attacked her raw knee, she hurriedly finished her first aid routine, threw her jeans in the hamper, and retreated to the comfort of her room.

The smell of cooking casserole wafted up from the kitchen as Denise, in underpants and a shirt, held onto her bedpost and attempted a grand plié. The tearing pain in her knee declared her absolutely unfit for ballet practice. Denise smirked. She knew her mom would understand. Her mom was okay. Both her parents were, not like poor Annie Wanamaker's.

What were Ruthie's parents like? She hardly ever spoke about them, except that her father was dead and had never let her go to synagogue. Why didn't Ruthie ever invite Denise home? Strange, very strange. And odd, how Ruthie somehow seemed unreal here at Denise's house, as if she couldn't possibly exist in this world, this cheerful, fooling-around but very loving and safe world.

Denise was standing in front of her open wardrobe trying to decide what to wear when her mother spoke.

"Are you *sure* you're okay, Pumpkin?"

"What?" Denise screamed in surprise, leaping behind her wardrobe door so that only her head poked out. Mrs Riley laughed.

"I'm sorry. I didn't mean to sneak up on you. I was just wondering if you weren't maybe hiding something from me."

"Only my body," Denise said, still shaking from the shock.

"You need a bra yet?" Mrs Riley asked, half-teasing.

"No, thank you."

"And there's really nothing you want to talk about?"

"Nothing. Honest, Mom."

Mrs Riley gave Denise a last piercing look, then sighed. "Very vell," she said in a husky voice. "I vill leaf you a-lawn." And she slouched out the door, her eyelids lowered and her mouth pursed like an old-time sexy movie star.

"Hey, Mom?" Denise called after her.

Mrs Riley peered around the doorway again. "Yessss? Vat isss it?"

"I love you."

At that, Mrs Riley blushed. A rosy flush crept from under her freckles to the roots of her red cap of curls. For a moment, she looked more like Denise's sister than her mother.

"Are you *sure* you're okay?" she asked.

Denise laughed and nodded her head.

But that night, Denise had a nightmare. It was about Ruthie, and it was a dream she would have over and over again in the next few months. In it, Ruthie appeared as a fawn, gentle, shy, and lovely. It wasn't Ruthie in a fawn costume or a fawn with Ruthie's face. It was a real fawn, but something in its sad eyes and the way it bobbed its delicate head convinced Denise, even as she dreamed, that it was Ruthie. The fawn kept trying to cross a brook that danced and sparkled in the sun, teasing and tempting the fawn with its gurgling brook voice. Where exactly the fawn wanted to go, Denise couldn't tell. She knew only that it desperately needed to get across and that something or someone important was waiting on the other side. Denise could feel the fawn's emotions in her dream. Even though the fawn was Ruthie, Denise saw everything from her point of view and it filled her with sadness and a miserable, helpless feeling. Every time the fawn approached the brook, a hunter appeared and frightened her away. He was a huge, stern man, old and grey and apparently furiously angry at the fawn. He never actually did anything to her, but every time he appeared, back into the woods she skittered on her fragile little legs. Again and again, she would try to reach the brook, until her eyes were wild with fear and longing and her tiny body trembled with exhaustion. She never made it.

Every morning, after having that dream, Denise would wake with a sense of doom. Something evil or unspeakably sad hung in the air all around her. The pit of her stomach felt queasy with dread. But of what? If Ruthie was the fawn, who was the hunter? Ruthie's father? But he was dead. And what had he done, anyway, to make him appear so terrifying? And what was waiting on the other side of the brook? Brook? Book? Cross a brook? Cross a book? Somehow it all had something to do with the stolen books. The answer was in there, Denise knew, without knowing why or how she knew. But days, weeks, and finally, months passed without Ruthie ever saying a word about them.

10

Ruthie knew something was terribly wrong. She had been trying, trying with all her might, to start her life over again. She hadn't touched the locket or the photographs or the books in months, although she hadn't been able to return the books to the library, either. The locket and photographs stayed in her mother's drawer, the books on her closet shelf, and all were pushed, forcefully, to the back of her mind. Whenever they threatened to break through, she hurriedly sketched a picture or called Denise on the phone or somehow busied herself until the thought disintegrated.

She began her bat mitzvah lessons and liked Rabbi Davis a lot. In some ways, he seemed nearly as shy as she was. He spoke softly and stuttered occasionally when he got really excited about a point he was trying to make. But he never, ever made her feel uncomfortable.

Aunt Sarah had mentioned that he was forty-eight years old and a widower, but he looked even older. He was tall and scrawny, as Aunt Sarah would say, a *"lange lukshen,"* a long noodle. There was a shiny bald spot right in the middle of his wispy blond hair and deep lines gave his slender face a weary look. His frequent smile always came as a surprise, as if he should always feel as forlorn as he appeared at first glance. But when you got close enough to study his brown eyes, enlarged and slightly distorted behind thick glasses, you saw the warmth and laughter there, as if life, for Rabbi Davis, were a bittersweet joke and he was glad he got it.

Ruthie sketched him twice: first, as a thin and rather

jittery ostrich; but later, when she had grown to love him, she drew him as he really was, a gentle man.

Ruthie studied the Hebrew blessings and the portion she was to read from the Torah fervently every day until Rabbi Davis said, his dark eyes gleaming with pride, that she was making excellent progress and would definitely be ready for the big day in June. With school, bat mitzvah lessons, Denise, and sketching, it wasn't hard to keep busy, but it was getting more and more difficult to keep busy *enough*.

Something was wrong inside her, she knew that. She was nervous all the time now, and watchful, as if expecting to be attacked without warning. Her attempts to keep busy were becoming frantic. And even worse, her day-dream about being Denise's sister was changing somehow. Where it had once held all the love and joy of Denise and her home, something new was slipping into it, a dark and evil stain.

Ruthie suspected that Denise knew something was wrong, too, although Denise was far too kind and thoughtful to come right out and say so. But there was a troubled expression on her face now and then. Ruthie caught it even though Denise tried to hide it. Often, a puzzled, concerned look would flicker in her eyes whenever Ruthie showed her a new drawing.

And they *were* different, the drawings. The humour had gone out of them. Instead, even though she pictured people as different, appropriate animals, as before, there was an anger in the pictures now, a hatefulness that surprised Ruthie herself. Frequently, when she looked at one of these new pictures, she felt as if someone else had drawn them. And when she drew, she was in a fog; it was as if someone else took the pencil—and the power—from her hand and arranged the deft, mocking strokes on the white page.

More and more, Ruthie hated to be alone. In private, her thoughts frightened her. She tried to arrive at school early and linger there as long as she could, or she spent more time at Denise's house or prowling the aisles at the supermarket.

74

The rabbi took to calling her his "ablebodied assistant" because she did odd jobs around the synagogue for him whenever she had nowhere else to go.

She didn't go there often, because she feared making a nuisance of herself, but she loved to be near Rabbi Davis. He never pried, or even questioned her presence; in fact, he seemed to enjoy it. It couldn't have been because he needed her help. Her unsteady, one-fingered typing made even the shortest letter or memo take practically forever. But something in the way he smiled whenever she appeared told her that, to him, Ruthie Morgenthau was a special person.

The less Ruthie wanted to be alone, the more she was. Aunt Sarah found that many of her wealthy friends were delighted to have an experienced tailor in their midst, so Ruthie's mother spent all her days and many evenings at Aunt Sarah's house, where she had arranged an airy, well-lighted sewing room around her ancient black machine with its squeaky foot pedal and gilded scroll-work. It was one of the few possessions from Boston they hadn't sold when they moved.

At night, almost every night now, Ruthie dreamed of running, chased by some dark, sinister force. In her dream, as in her life, the more she ran, the more she seemed to be losing ground.

There were days when she wanted to confide in someone so badly her throat and chest ached. But who would listen and understand? She would never, ever burden her mother with it; her mother had suffered enough. She still felt shy with the rabbi, and, anyway, she wanted his praise, not his pity. Aunt Sarah was so excited about the bat mitzvah and her mother's new tailoring customers, Ruthie couldn't bear to disturb her, either. There were times when she almost, oh-so-nearly almost, confessed all her fears and confusion to Denise. But where would she begin? How could she possibly make Denise understand?

Besides, *not* talking about it was the whole point. This was supposed to be her new life, her fresh, clean start. She couldn't bring the filth of the past into it. It would spoil everything. It would turn everything sour. She had to go on, running, stumbling, doing the best she could. She had to go on.

One bleak March afternoon, Ruthie arrived home from school and let herself into the house. There never seemed to be a change of seasons there, certainly not a spring. It was always evening, too, amidst the heavy, dark furniture, and always, even on the most sunshiny, bird-singing days, something of November's grey emptiness.

Ruthie knew her mother would not be home that night. She was very busy with her sewing, putting the finishing touches on a dozen gowns for the gala Deerfield Charity Ball held each spring. She intended to work as late as she could, spend the night at Aunt Sarah's, and start in again early in the morning. According to Aunt Sarah, the rich ladies of Deerfield, with the help of Hannah's "golden touch," were going to look sublime.

Ruthie took a banana off the kitchen counter and left her school books in its place. Casting about for something to do, she remembered the tape recorder the rabbi had loaned her. She was supposed to listen to the Hebrew blessings as he chanted them, and then try to imitate his every inflection. She took the banana and the tape recorder to her room. After plugging in the recorder, she set it beside her on the bed and pressed the start button. She listened to the familiar voice as she peeled her banana. Rabbi Davis never stuttered when he chanted blessings. From somewhere deep in his skinny rib cage came a booming baritone voice, as surprising as his sudden grins. Alone in her room, Ruthie couldn't help but smile as she listened.

"Ba-re-chu et A-do-nai ha-me-vo-rach!" Praise the Lord, to whom our praise is due!

"Ba-ruch A-do-nai ha-me-vo-rach le-o-lam va-ed!"

Praised be the Lord, to whom our praise is due, now and forever!

"Ba–ruch a–ta, A–do–nai E–lo–hei–nu, me–lech ha–o–lam . . ."

Ruthie listened to the tape twice through. Then, stuffing in the last of her banana, she decided she was ready to chant along. She ran back the tape and began.

"Ba–re–chu et A–do–nai ha–me–vo–rach! Ba–ruch A–do–nai . . ."

Suddenly, she switched off the recorder and held her breath. What had she heard? Voices? Yes, *voices*! There, along with the rabbi's rich nasal chant and her own piping efforts, were *other voices*, a chorus of voices chanting in the distance. It had sounded to Ruthie like the wailing of a thousand ghosts.

With a little cry, she leaped off her bed and ran into the kitchen. Her fingers shook as she quickly dialled Denise's number. Two rings, three rings, four. Oh, *please* answer, Denise, *please*.

"Hello?"

"Denise?"

"Uh-huh. Is that you, Ruthie?"

"Yeah. Um . . . listen . . . uh, my mother's not going to be home tonight, and, um, I was wondering if you could spend the night here? You know, keep me company?"

"Oh, sure. I'd love to. I mean, if my mom says okay. I think she will. Hold on a second."

Hold on, Ruthie told herself, listening to the clumping of the phone receiver against the wall where Denise had left it dangling. She could hear footsteps and Denise calling to her mother.

"Mom? Mooo–ooom?"

"What?" came the reply from a different direction.

"It's Ruthie. Can I spend the night at her house? Her Mom's not home and she's all alone. She wants company."

"What?"

"Oh, for pity's sake. Where are you?"

"What? Come here a minute. Where are *you*?"

"I'm right here!"

Listening on the other end of the line as Denise and Mrs Riley found each other, Ruthie didn't know whether to laugh or cry. Everything was so simple at Denise's house. There was always laughter and silliness. Silliness. In all her life, Ruthie had never once seen her parents act silly. She could not, no matter how hard she tried, ever imagine either of them giggling.

"Okay, I'm coming," Denise suddenly announced into the phone.

"Oh, good."

"Anything special you want me to bring?"

"No," Ruthie replied. Only yourself, she thought, now much closer to tears than to laughter.

"Okay. See ya soon."

Ruthie knew immediately that Denise's presence wasn't going to end her problem. Even while Denise sat chattering across the shadowed living room, spasms of anxiety, like an electric current, charged through her veins. It was too much. She could not go on like this.

"You want to do our hair?" Denise was asking. "I brought my dryer. Well, actually it's my mom's. I just let mine dry. What's the sense fighting it? But my mom found this new way to blow out her curls . . ."

Ruthie shook her head. "I want to show you something," she said, her voice so husky she hardly recognised it herself.

Trembling, she stood up and walked into her mother's bedroom, only vaguely aware that Denise was following her. She watched her own hands, oddly disconnected from herself, open the middle drawer of her mother's dresser and remove the jewellery box. In a moment, the open locket dangled on its chain from her fingers. Denise reached out and cupped it in her hand. She peered at the picture, tilting it towards the light to see better. A little girl gazed up at her, but the photograph was too faded to see well.

"Is that you?" Denise asked.

"My sister," Ruthie said.

"I didn't know you had a sister. I mean, I thought I was your sister, kind of . . ."

"She's dead. She died in Poland, in a German concentration camp."

"Oh," Denise whispered, her face flooded with concern. "I'm sorry."

"It was a long time ago. Almost thirty years. It wouldn't really have been like having a sister. She would have been old enough to be my mother. I don't know very much about her. She was very young when she died. Three or four, maybe, I'm not sure."

Ruthie didn't look at Denise. It didn't matter if she wanted to listen or not. It was all going to come out. There was no more holding it back.

"My parents are survivors of concentration camps. They never talk to me about it. I used to ask questions when I was little, but I don't anymore. But I used to hear my mother and Aunt Sarah talking about it, sometimes, late at night. They thought I was asleep. I wasn't. I'd sneak into the hallway and huddle in the dark, listening. Part of me didn't want to hear and yet I couldn't move. I *had* to listen. I didn't sleep at all those nights, even after they stopped talking. I didn't understand half of the things they talked about. Sometimes they spoke Yiddish or German. But I could *sense* the meaning of it, the hate and humiliation and fear. I don't know exactly what my mother went through. I wish I did. I imagine *everything*. I see her beaten and starved and raped. *My* mother. They may have done that to *my* mother. And other people, too, millions of them. Not just Jews. Catholics, gypsies, anybody they wanted. Can you imagine it? I watch her sometimes at her sewing machine, concentrating

79

with all her might, turning out such lovely things with her quick hands. And I think of what she must have seen and suffered. It seems impossible. Why would anyone want to hurt *her*? But they did. They hurt her terribly. So terribly, she won't tell me any of it.

"And they killed her baby, that I know for sure, although she said very little about it, even to Aunt Sarah. Never anything about how she died or what she was like. Just a little girl, I guess. An ordinary little girl. Except . . . the odd thing is, though . . . sometimes . . ."

Ruthie's voice trailed off. This was unbearable, this pain was so deep, talking about it was like ripping her insides apart. Before her, Denise stood perfectly still, the locket still resting in her open palm.

"The odd thing is," Ruthie went on, choking on her words, "sometimes it seems like she's more alive than I am. I've seen my mother crying over that locket. She doesn't even know I know about it. And I've seen her . . . often . . . daydreaming . . . and I think she's thinking about that girl. Her daughter. My sister. She never cries over me. She never . . . really *looks* at me. Sometimes I begin to think I'm invisible. What I want, what I need, what I feel is nothing compared to what they suffered. My mother's pain is so huge it fills every room and covers me completely. It leaves me no space, no air to breathe. If only I could make it up to her. If only I could just once see her smiling and happy like your mother is every day."

Suddenly, Ruthie pulled out the flat box and pushed back its lid. She heard Denise gasp as the photographs scattered across the dresser. There were bodies, tangled heaps of naked, skeletal human bodies. And faces, horrible sunken cheeks and enormous, luminous, suffering eyes. Had her parents looked like this once? Had her sister looked like this before she died? Ruthie touched first one face, then another, gently, softly, as if caressing a sleeping child. All at once, great aching sobs ripped through her and she slumped forward over the photographs, bathing them with her tears. She felt Denise's arms around her. Her cries shook them both as they clung to each other.

11

"I haven't told you everything," Ruthie said suddenly.

Denise sat bolt upright in bed. She'd just dozed off and Ruthie's voice came as such a surprise her heart raced in panic.

"What?"

"I'm sorry. I thought you were still awake. I said I haven't told you everything. Do you mind if I turn on the light?"

"No. Go ahead."

Ruthie slid out of the lumpy double bed and in a minute the room was filled with a yellow glare. Denise yawned and rubbed her eyes. They ached as if something inside her head were pushing against them, trying to pop them right out of their sockets.

It had been an incredible evening, with Ruthie talking and crying as if she would never stop. Denise was exhausted. Now Ruthie was rummaging around on the shelf in her closet. In a moment, she had tossed three books on the bed in front of Denise. The library books!

"I took these from the library. I guess I stole them. I didn't check them out."

Denise looked away, ashamed as if she, not Ruthie, had done the stealing. "I know," she admitted. "I saw you put them in your bag."

"You saw and you didn't say anything?"

"What could I say?"

Ruthie shrugged. "I guess you wondered why I did it."

"Sure. But if you'd wanted to tell me, you would have."

Ruthie sat on the bed, facing Denise, and pushed the books across to her. Denise saw immediately that they were all about the Holocaust. She riffled through the pages and saw more pictures like the gory photographs buried in Mrs Morgenthau's dresser.

"Sometimes I want to know all about it," Ruthie mused, "everything, every disgusting detail, every drop of blood, every tear, every charred inch of human skin. I want to fill myself up with it, like a poison, until I choke. Or explode into a million pieces. And other times, I want to pretend it never happened at all.

"I told you my parents never talked to me about it. It was worse than that. My father would fly into crazy rages if anyone even mentioned it in front of him. He would curse God and then deny there was ever a God. 'What kind of God would permit this?' he'd howl. And he'd lash out and kick things and pound holes in the walls with his bare fists. Tears flew from his eyes. It was terrifying. He was so full of anger, he seemed to be burning up with it. I'd run and hide under the table. But my mother would sit there with her head bowed, perfectly still and alone, like the eye of a hurricane. Afterwards, they wouldn't speak at all, for days sometimes. Not to each other, not to me. I learned never to ask questions—about anything. And yet, I remember, even as a little girl, I thought there *had* to be a God. Because nobody could be so furious at something that didn't even exist. I never, ever talked about it to anyone. Except Aunt Sarah, a little bit, when no one else was around. Sometimes Aunt Sarah would lie to him and sneak me off to synagogue, but it would make me so nervous, I'd cry. Papa didn't even want me to play with the other kids in our neighbourhood because they were Jewish. He hated being Jewish, hated everything to do with it, because of what happened to him, I guess. I went to school alone and I came home alone. I was afraid to make friends. For the longest time, I thought

83

everybody's house was like ours, filled with sadness and
anger and silence. Then, as I got older, I thought, Aunt
Sarah's house couldn't be like ours. And I'd read books
about families not like ours. Jewish families, even. But it
wasn't till we moved here and I saw your house that I knew
for sure how it could be."

Denise smiled, but something about Ruthie's faith in her
family bothered her. It was as if she and her parents had been
given too much responsibility, as if Ruthie were asking
them always to be happy, perfectly happy, for her sake.
Denise knew they weren't really like that. Nobody's *perfectly* happy, she wanted to tell Ruthie. We have stomach aches
and bad moods like everyone else. But in one way, Ruthie
was right: nothing the Rileys suffered was anywhere near
equal to what the Morgenthaus had been through. She
studied Ruthie curiously, trying to imagine her strange life
in Boston, just as Ruthie must have studied her own
mother, so far from the nightmares of the war and yet
carrying scars forever. Denise thought she understood,
maybe just a little, how much Ruthie yearned to make it all
up to Mrs Morgenthau, because she, too, wished somehow
to erase all the pain for Ruthie. But how could she? What
could she possibly do?

Ruthie sighed and flipped the pages of a book absently.

"Anyway," she went on, "that's why I took the books. It
was one of those days when I wanted to drown myself in
the agony of it. But . . . this sounds really crazy, but it's
true . . . I thought my father would know if I checked
them out, so I didn't. I just took them."

"How could he know? He's dead."

Ruthie tapped her chest, over her heart. "Inside of me,
he's not dead. None of them are. I hear them all the time.
Wherever I go, whatever I do, I hear them and they're
never, ever pleased. My father would hate my bat mitzvah;
a thousand ghosts before him would say I don't deserve it.
Why should I live and celebrate when they suffered and

died? On the other hand, Aunt Sarah is wild with joy about it. And my mother . . . I don't know. She said she wanted it, so I'm doing it more for her than anyone. But she goes on as she always has, as if she and I were living on separate clouds, floating near each other sometimes, but never together. I want so much to make her happy. But I'm afraid. I'm so afraid. It's like a whole country is living inside me and they're all warring over what I ought to be doing. And no matter what I finally do, it's never right for everyone. It's never enough."

Ruthie flipped the books shut and put them back onto the shelf. A thought flickered through Denise's mind, a quote she'd copied into her notebook long ago: "The evil men do dies with them." Where did that come from? The Bible? Ben Franklin? Somebody. Well, whoever it was, was wrong. The evil goes on and on, secretly, stealthily, hurting people again and again. Couldn't anything stop it? Wasn't there somewhere a good enormous enough to wipe out the evil forever?

"I'll return the books for you, Ruthie," she offered. "Don't worry about them, okay? I'll just drop them in the night deposit box."

"Thanks, Denise."

That much she could do. But what a very little thing it was.

Denise was still awake, pondering all that had happened, when Ruthie stirred beside her and moaned in her sleep. Denise patted her shoulder to comfort her, but instead, Ruthie cried out and began thrashing her arms and legs. In a moment, she had thrown the blanket off the bed and was sitting up, wild-eyed with something far beyond fear.

"Ruthie, are you all right?"

"Rachel?"

"What? Ruthie, it's me, Denise. What's wrong?"

"Rachel! You're home! You're *home*. I knew it. I *knew* you'd come back. I'll tell Mama. Wait here. I'll tell her."

85

Denise watched in horror as Ruthie slipped off the bed and stumbled towards the door, calling her mother. Who was Rachel? It had to be her sister, her poor, lost little sister of long ago.

Denise leaped off the bed and caught Ruthie's arm.

"Ruthie, wait. What are you doing? I'm not Rachel. I'm Denise. Can't you see?"

Ruthie struggled free of Denise's grip. Although her eyes were gleaming in the dark, they seemed unfocused. She stroked Denise's face as a blind person might.

"She'll be so happy. Mama will be so happy. You're home. You're really home. She'll be so happy."

Freezing waves shivered down Denise's spine each time Ruthie's fingertips touched her. She grasped Ruthie's hand in both of hers and screamed into her face: "Stop it! Stop it, *please*, Ruthie! It's *me*. It's *Denise*. I'm not your sister. I'd give anything in the world to be Rachel for you, but I'm not. Now, stop it, you're frightening me. *Please!*"

For a second, Ruthie stared back at her, then her whole body began to shudder so hard, her teeth chattered.

"Denise?" she managed to whimper.

Denise helped her back to the bed and turned on the light. Ruthie blinked and clumsily tried to pull the blanket around her shoulders. Denise covered her, then stood back, unsure of what to do next. She touched her hand to Ruthie's cheek. It felt ice cold.

The light and the blanket's warmth finally calmed Ruthie.

"I'm sorry," she whispered. "I know I had a nightmare. It happens sometimes."

"That's okay," Denise answered, sitting beside her. "I just wish you didn't have to suffer so. I wish there was something I could do to help you."

"You've already done it," Ruthie said, with a weary smile. "I *talked* to you, I *told* you. Everything. As much as I know, anyway. You don't know what that means to me,

86

having somebody who has heard the whole miserable story. You're not going to believe this, but I feel better now. I really do."

"I'm glad," Denise said. Huddled close to Ruthie, Denise felt warmth flowing back into Ruthie's limbs again. For just this little while, there seemed to be enough good, enough love between them, to keep the evil at bay.

When Denise dragged herself home the next morning, her parents took one look at her droopy shoulders and red-rimmed eyes and burst into laughter.

"You look awful," her mother cried. "I'll bet you two didn't sleep a wink."

"Well, maybe a wink," Denise said, stumbling over the rocker before collapsing into an easy chair.

"Up all night gabbing," Mr Riley said.

"Hm-hmmm," Denise admitted, curling up drowsily. "Up all night gabbing."

Her last waking thought was that it was so good to be home where her mother quietly tucked a blanket around her and war and hatred and fear almost seemed impossible.

12

"Are you sure you don't want to come, Mama?" Ruthie asked, trying to sound sincere. "The Rileys have been wanting to meet you for months."

"No, no," Mrs Morgenthau insisted in her quiet but immovable way. She waved Ruthie towards the door. "It will be too much for me. I'm nervous enough without meeting new people, too. You go and then tell me all about it. Please."

"But I don't like to leave you alone. And aren't you at all curious? I mean, Aunt Sarah is going to be *interviewed* on *television*. All by herself. Just *her*. Don't you want to hear what she says?"

Mrs Morgenthau chewed a finger pensively. From her seat at the kitchen table, heaped with bits of cloth and sequins like tiny brilliant coloured puddles, she eyed the window over the sink as if waiting for a decision to appear there.

"No," she said again and Ruthie knew it was final. "Please, no. You go and report."

Ruthie drew a deep breath, partly in disappointment and partly in relief. She planted a kiss on her mother's wrinkled cheek, then left as quickly as she decently could, an umbrella shielding her against the April drizzle, but not against the jumble of conflicting emotions churning in her stomach.

From the time Aunt Sarah had told them about the interview and the Rileys had invited them to watch it on their colour TV, she had been in turmoil. At the Rileys' house, she was a normal, twelve-year-old kid, perhaps a bit shy, but with no greater problem than what another scoop of chocolate ice cream might do to her complexion. The Rileys knew nothing of her bizarre family history and she wanted to keep it that way. She dreaded the day they would meet her mother and know, without a word being spoken, that she came from another, darker world and that a part of her was still there, permanently trapped in memories.

Ruthie wanted to put that meeting off as long as possible, forever, if she could. She wanted to go on pretending she was part of the Riley household and bask in its sunshine for as long as they would let her. She feared that her background would make them pity her, and that would dim the sunshine for good.

Today, as she walked briskly towards Denise's house, the privilege of spending time there seemed more precious than ever, because it had come so close to being spoiled by her mother's presence. Ruthie shrugged off the twinge of guilt that thought evoked and hurried on her way.

Ever since that night, nearly a month ago, when she had confessed to Denise, she had been feeling better and stronger than ever before in her whole life. Her schoolwork was going well. And the closer she and Denise became, the more the rest of the class seemed to accept them. It was almost as if, now that they weren't *desperate* for friends, the others were more willing to be friendly. Even Maxine had given up trying to belittle them. All her energy was geared towards being elected Sigma Iota Princess at the Spring Fling. Denise thought that was the stupidest goal any woman could ever set for herself, although she only expressed that opinion in private to Ruthie. Ruthie thought that, just maybe, Denise was a little bit jealous. Todd Jones's brother was a Sigma Iota and Todd was pretty impressed with Maxine's popularity with the high school crowd.

Denise was bouncing up and down on the porch as

Ruthie rounded the corner. She dashed down the block to meet Ruthie.

"Come on, come on. The news is on. Will you hurry? You're going to miss it. Run, for Pete's sake, *run*." The two broke into a trot.

"You think Maxine's watching?" Denise asked.

"I doubt it. Tonight's Spring Fling."

"Oh, that's right. Weirdo's delight."

Inside the house, Mr and Mrs Riley were already seated on the sofa. The flickering TV, on its rolling stand, had been pulled up especially close for the occasion.

"We'll probably get radiation poisoning," Denise puffed as she and Ruthie collapsed on the gold carpet in front of the sofa.

"Shhhh!" her mother warned her.

The interviewer appeared on the screen. She was a petite elfin creature who looked much too young for the job. Mr Riley hunched forward, his eyes squinted in puzzlement.

"That's a new one," he said. "I wonder where the regulars are."

"Good evening," the new woman—girl, really— squeaked. "I'm Jocelyn Rogers and this is Deerfield Update. As you know, each week we interview a prominent Deerfieldian on an important issue affecting our community."

Butterflies jumped around in Ruthie's stomach. But even she, in her excited state, could see that the most nervous person so far was Jocelyn Rogers.

"She's reading the introduction off cue cards," Mrs Riley exclaimed. "Look! You can see her eyes moving from left to right!"

"She must be just an office girl or something," Mr Riley said. "But why'd they give her an important interview the first time out?"

"Shhhhh!" Denise hissed. "She's introducing Aunt Sarah."

"As you know," Jocelyn Rogers went on, "municipal elections will be held next Tuesday. One of the most controversial issues facing the voters will be that of deciding whether or not to sell ten acres of undeveloped land on the northeast side of the city. The land, as most of you know, was willed to the city by the late Foster L. Marymount, whose family settled there in 1843 and farmed the land until Mr Marymount made his fortune in the ammunition industry during World War II. A bid for the land has been made by Fitzhugh Development Corporation. And one of our most outspoken council members, Mrs Sarah Abrams, is here with us tonight to give her comments on the issue."

Ruthie's insides somersaulted the moment Aunt Sarah's name was mentioned. She and Denise held hands tightly as the camera pulled back to reveal Aunt Sarah seated beside Jocelyn Rogers. She looked absolutely dazzling, her great big smile framed in turquoise paisley and the shining silver of her hair. Unlike the interviewer, she didn't seem one bit nervous. In fact, she looked like she *belonged* right there on television, maybe even on the Tonight show. By the time she'd spoken her first sentence, Ruthie and Denise were hugging each other and giggling uncontrollably.

"Shhhhhhhh!" Mr Riley insisted, but his eyes were gleaming.

It was all Ruthie could do to stop thinking about how wonderful Aunt Sarah looked and to concentrate on what she was saying.

"Mrs Abrams," the interviewer said, or rather, *read* off the cue card, "you've lived in Deerfield quite a long time."

"Yes, I have. I came here in 1938 with my husband, Izzy, God rest his soul. We were among the founders of Temple Beth Israel. There were less than a dozen Jewish families here at the time."

"That would be thirty-five years ago."

"That's correct."

"And how long have you served on the city council?"

"I decided to run for office the year my husband passed away. That was 1969, so about four years. Serving on the Deerfield city council has given me a renewed interest in life. I hope I have given Deerfield back something as well."

"I think you have. I really do, Mrs Abrams," Jocelyn Rogers blurted out earnestly, forgetting herself and the cue cards for a moment. While Aunt Sarah graciously thanked her, the poor young woman squinted towards the camera, trying to find her place in the script again. There was a desperate moment of silence. Ruthie and the Rileys held their breath, silently urging on poor Ms Rogers. But Aunt Sarah just smiled into the camera as if there was nothing she enjoyed more than sitting in a TV studio in front of thousands of Deerfieldians, beside a panicked interviewer.

"Ah . . . ah . . . where do you stand . . . um . . . Mrs . . . ah . . . Abrams, on the sale of the city property near the northeast boundary?"

"I'm against it," Aunt Sarah said, firmly.

"Are you against it on principle, or because the Fitzhugh Corporation is the only bidder at this time?"

"I would prefer more bidders."

"So that, perhaps, the city would profit more from the sale."

"Among other reasons."

"Are you aware," Ms Rogers pressed on, somewhat more composed, "that some people feel you are waging a personal vendetta against the Fitzhugh Corporation?"

"I'm aware that some people think so. But I have nothing against the Fitzhugh Corporation *personally*. I don't even know them personally. They may be very charming people. If I *am* waging a vendetta, it's against inferior craftsmanship. I feel it is inexcusable. In a country so rich and so knowledgeable, the standard need never be lower than absolute excellence."

92

Jocelyn Rogers blinked, a look of utter adoration flooding her face. "Would you elaborate on that idea?" she asked, worshipfully.

Aunt Sarah obliged.

"I have a sister-in-law who designs and tailors clothing with such meticulous attention to detail it does my heart good to hold a piece of her work in my hands. She has neither the wealth nor the power of a giant development corporation, but she has pride in her work and she is dedicated to perfection."

"She's talking about your mother!" Denise squealed. She hugged Ruthie so hard, Ruthie's nose got mashed. For the rest of the interview, Ruthie couldn't tell if the stinging tears in her eyes were from pain or pride.

"My sister-in-law, Hannah Morgenthau," Aunt Sarah went on, "would rather do an extra day's work for no pay at all than present her customers with something less than they deserve. To me, her attitude and her work show a great respect for humanity. And, in contrast, those who offer their customers inferior goods show nothing but disdain for human dignity, their own as well as their customers'. They may fool some of the people some of the time, but they insult us all, all of the time."

The camera, which had pulled in so close to Aunt Sarah that her face filled the screen, now rolled back. Into the picture came Jocelyn Rogers, hunched towards Aunt Sarah with her eyes and mouth wide open. Someone offscreen must have given her a signal because she suddenly straightened up as if jolted out of a deep trance.

"Um . . . um . . . um . . ." she faltered, "ah . . . when you say these development corporations, Mrs Abrams, are you referring specifically to Fitzhugh?"

Aunt Sarah folded her hands in her lap in a quietly defiant gesture. "If the shoe fits," she said.

"Mrs Abrams, are you saying that buildings constructed by Fitzhugh are unsafe?"

"That I'm not sure of. The building code inspector is inspecting, thanks to pressure from yours truly."

The programme cut to a commercial and Denise leaped to her feet, bowling Ruthie over and whooping wildly.

"She was terrific, wasn't she? Mom? Dad? *Say* something! Wasn't she amazing? She's like . . . she's like a . . . a knight in shining armour! Only she's a *woman*. Joan of Arc! Joan of Arc rides again! Oh, Ruthie, when am I going to meet her in person? Huh? I want her autograph. I really do. I think she should run for President of the United States."

Ruthie had to laugh at Denise, but she didn't share her unabashed approval of Aunt Sarah. She wasn't exactly sure why, but Aunt Sarah's outspokenness on everything, including her religion, made Ruthie uncomfortable, fearful. Aunt Sarah was so fiery, she made enemies, powerful enemies. Mr Riley immediately confirmed her fears. As soon as the interview set was replaced by the weather map, he flipped off the TV and rolled it back to the wall.

"Well," he said, "now we know why they gave that interview to a novice. The old hands knew it was a hot potato and they weren't about to handle it. Mr Fitzhugh is one powerful man around this town."

"Aunt Sarah can handle him," Denise crowed.

But Ruthie sensed concern from the older Rileys.

"What do you think?" Mrs Riley asked her husband.

"I really don't know," he admitted. "It's a tough question. Very complex."

"What do you mean, you don't know?" Denise howled. "Aunt Sarah's right. She's *always* right."

Mrs Riley laughed. "Oh, Denise, everything's so simple for you. Heroes and villians, right and wrong, good and evil." She shook her head, as if she wondered if Denise were hopeless. Then she turned her attention to Ruthie. "We must get together with your mother and aunt, Ruthie. We've wanted to meet them for so long."

For a long moment, a silence hung in the air that

94

quietened even Denise. Ruthie stammered, "I know, but . . . well, they're busy. The election and all."

"Well, right after the election, I'm going to call them and invite them for dinner. Even celebrities have to eat!"

That evening, Ruthie and her mother, not the Rileys, dined with the celebrity. An exuberant Aunt Sarah called to invite them to a triumphant dinner for three. When they arrived, in the midst of a thunderstorm, six long blue candles flickered on the table. Their glow was nothing next to Aunt Sarah's. She looked so alive, so young, so victorious, that Ruthie's vague fears were replaced by daydreams about Aunt Sarah's past. She must have been like this, and quite beautiful, too, as a young girl in Germany. Ruthie imagined her as something of a flirt. Not a blatant one, like Maxine, but one with a flowerlike sweetness around which boys must have gathered like bees. Uncle Izzy probably considered himself the luckiest man in the world when he won Aunt Sarah for himself. And he *was* lucky. They both were. They left Germany before the war. Why hadn't her parents gone, too, while they had the chance? That one decision had made all the difference. Because of it, Ruthie's parents gave not the slightest hint of having ever been young and carefree and in love. They *must* have had dreams for the future and happy memories like other people did. They must have gone to school and had friends. And yet it seemed impossible. Try as she might, Ruthie could not imagine her parents as children: playing games, scraping knees, sharing secrets. As far as she could tell, they had always been old and sad, and their secrets were unsharable.

The next morning, Sunday, Ruthie was awakened by her mother's cries. They weren't the usual haunted screams of her nightmares. Her voice was coming from the kitchen. Had the phone been ringing or had Ruthie only dreamed it? She climbed out of bed groggily and padded into the kitchen.

Immediately, her mother waved the phone towards her. "It's Sarah. You talk. In the hospital."

"The hospital?" Ruthie grabbed the phone. "Aunt Sarah? It's Ruthie. What happened?"

"Please don't get all excited, sweetheart. And try to keep your mama calm. I was out in the yard gathering some limbs the storm had blown down and someone threw a rock over my fence. It hit me on the head. I'm going to need some stitches. I'm in the emergency room now. It may take a while."

"We'll be right down."

"I appreciate it, but only if your mother feels she's able. I don't want her all upset; it's not that bad."

"We'll be right down, Aunt Sarah. We'll take a cab. Good-bye."

But Ruthie could see immediately that it *was* going to be hard. Her mother, who was rocking back and forth in her chair and wringing her hands together, looked shrivelled to half her normal size. Everyday life was hard enough for her, but emergencies were more than she could stand. The sound of a siren terrified her; a loud knock on the door could throw her into a panic. Now, Ruthie spoke to her softly, handling her gently as she'd learned to do almost as soon as she had learned to walk and talk. Other children might shout at their mothers impatiently, or throw temper tantrums in frustration, but Ruthie had learned to control herself and to treat her mother as if she were the most fragile of dolls. At times like these, when ancient fears became overwhelming, Ruthie knew that *she* must be the adult, no matter how badly she herself might long for reassurance.

"Mama," she said, "the taxi will be here any minute. I'd like you to come with me. I don't want you to stay here alone."

Mrs Morgenthau nodded, without looking at Ruthie. Her thin lips moved in what appeared to be a silently repeated prayer.

Ruthie parted the curtains at the front window. The sun was shining, sparkling brilliantly on the wet grass. Ruthie refused to think of Aunt Sarah, of how and why she'd been hurt. Instead, she concentrated all her energies on doing whatever had to be done, calmly, without emotion, especially without panic.

A yellow taxi pulled up at the curb and sounded two short beeps on its horn. Ruthie cupped her mother's elbow in her hand and steered her out of the house.

The emergency room of Deerfield General Hospital gleamed cold and efficient in the clear morning light. The nurses' fixed smiles, their hurried steps, their stiff uniforms and spotless white shoes gave them a robot-like appearance and the room an aura of unreal, futuristic space drama. As the receptionist led Ruthie and Mrs Morgenthau through a maze of small cubicles divided by creased green curtains, Ruthie had to remind herself of why they had come. She was still struggling with the unreality of it all, when Aunt Sarah waved to them from flat on her back on an examining table, and Mrs Morgenthau fainted.

In a split second, three nurses had surrounded Mrs Morgenthau.

"She has a bad heart," Ruthie heard herself saying. Everything seemed to be happening on the far side of a heavy mist, but she forced herself to hang on, to function, because her mother needed her.

She stood by her mother while the young resident on duty examined her. She gave the necessary information to the admitting clerk. She followed the orderlies as they wheeled her mother to a room and lifted her onto a bed.

"It's not her heart," the resident informed Ruthie, as if she were an adult, as if she weren't shaking from head to toe. "I've given her a mild tranquillizer. She'll sleep for a while. Your aunt's internist will have some tests run later. Maybe you'd better go home with your aunt. She's been released and you both look like you need some rest. Come back in a few hours. Your mother won't even know you're gone."

Still moving through a haze, Ruthie found her way back to the emergency room. Aunt Sarah was sitting on the edge of the table now and, for the first time, Ruthie realised what had frightened her mother so: without makeup, with half her beautiful hair shaved and replaced by bandages, Aunt Sarah looked haggard and hurt, like the people in the hidden photographs, the people who had suffered like her mother.

Feeling as robot-like as the nurses in the emergency room, Ruthie insisted on seeing Aunt Sarah home safely, but refused to stay there once Aunt Sarah's housekeeper had taken over. Instead, she stopped at her own house to pack her mother's nightgown and toothbrush, then returned to the hospital to sit for hours at her mother's bedside, comforting her. Despite her mother's questions, she evaded the full story of what had happened to Aunt Sarah. She'd listened on the way home, but her mind refused to register the meaning of the words. Their ugliness meant nothing at all; they might just as well have been spoken in another language.

In the evening, after Mrs Morgenthau had been given another injection, Ruthie went home and collapsed into bed, exhausted and still too numb to cry.

13

It was unusually quiet at the Riley's house, even for a Sunday evening. Mr Riley was away, at his lab, waiting with his infinite patience for some small but long-hoped for chemical reaction to take place. Mrs Riley was in the backyard, gathering laundry off the line. Denise was lolling on the porch swing, sucking a popsicle, when the newspaper boy drove up and hurled the evening paper into the neighbours' hedge.

"What a creep," Denise muttered to herself, stretching lazily before moving to retrieve the paper. Why he couldn't walk like normal paperboys—paperpeople?—she'd never understand. It wasn't that he *couldn't* walk; he made it up to the door just fine when he was collecting money. But he insisted on showing off his jeep, starting and stopping as noisily as possible and tossing papers like hand grenades, all to the beat of a deafening rock and roll radio station. What a cree . . .

"Oh, my God!" Denise screamed. "Mom! Mom!"

She tossed away the popsicle and let the screen door slam behind her as she dashed into the house.

"Mom? Mom! Ruthie's Aunt Sarah's been hurt! Look!" The house echoed emptily. Denise raced to the back door and out into the yard, repeating her message for all the world to hear.

A pink nightgown fluttered to the ground unnoticed as Mrs Riley snatched the newspaper from Denise's hand. There was Aunt Sarah's picture on page one. She was pressing a towel to her head as a nurse led her into the

99

emergency entrance of Deerfield General.

"Somebody threw a rock over her fence," Mrs Riley read. "A man. She heard him shout . . . something."

"What?" Denise asked, urgently.

"Oh . . . well, it was about the northeast property."

Denise knew her mother was holding something back. And it was something awful, too, because the colour had drained from her face, leaving her sprinkle of freckles startlingly dark.

"What did he say? Was it Mr Fitzhugh? Tell me, or I'll just read it myself."

Relenting, Mrs Riley handed Denise the paper. She read:

"A deeply troubled Mrs Abrams told Officer Kramer that the rock thrower had shouted, 'Stay off the northeast property, Jew bastard.'"

Denise's blue eyes widened with dismay. "Mom, why would he say a thing like that? What does her religion have to do with the northeast property?"

Mrs Riley sighed and shook her head sadly. "People are just cruel sometimes, Denise. Thoughtless and ignorant and cruel."

Denise felt hot tears welling in her eyes. "If I could just get a hold of that guy, whoever he is, no matter how big and tough, I'd kill him. I would. I'd claw his eyes out first. I'd . . ."

Mrs Riley draped a comforting arm over Denise's shoulder and brushed a light kiss across her curly head. "Oh, Pumpkin, I know you're angry. So am I. But what good would *that* do?"

"Well, we have to do *something*."

"We'll go over to Ruthie's house and see if we can make ourselves useful. That's probably a better idea than murder, don't you think?"

"I'm not so sure," Denise muttered, but the fury inside her was already giving way to concern about Ruthie and her family.

"Does it say in the article if her aunt is still in the hospital?" she wondered.

Mrs Riley skimmed through the article, spotted Hannah Morgenthau's name and discovered the rest of the story. Realising that Ruthie might be all alone, she and Denise hurried into their ageing orange Toyota and sped away, Denise directing her mother over the familiar northward route.

Both the front and back doors of Ruthie's house were locked. The curtains were drawn, giving the impression that the house was deserted. But Denise pounded impatiently, first on the doors, then on a window.

"Ruthie!" she shouted. "It's me. Denise. Are you okay? Ruthie!"

"Hey! What the hell's going on down there?"

Denise and her mother jumped in surprise, practically into each other's arms. Leaning from a second-floor window of the house next door was a grey-headed man. His hair stood up in points all over his head and glinted in the fading light like a steel crown. He was unshaven and furious.

"What's all the racket about?" he growled.

"We're very sorry to disturb you," Mrs Riley said, "but it's an emergency. We're looking for Ruthie Morgenthau. Have you seen her?"

"Never heard of her. Look, lady, I been working split shift all week. This is the first good sleep I've had. I ain't seen no Ruthies or Brucies or whatever. Now, will you hold it down? Or do I have to call the police?"

"Yes, sir!" Mrs Riley said, rolling her eyes in disgust.

The robe-clad figure disappeared, slamming the window shut behind him. Denise wondered if that could be the monster who'd thrown the rock at Aunt Sarah. Somebody just like him, probably. How could human beings be so *inhuman*?

Then, to her surprise, Ruthie opened the front door.

101

"Ruthie!" Denise cried, then clamped a hand over her mouth, remembering the angry neighbour. "Are you all right?" she went on, her voice hushed.

Ruthie nodded, but she certainly didn't look all right. Her ordinarily pale face was ashen and her dark eyes were sunk into deep, gaunt circles.

"We came over to see if there was anything we could do, Ruthie," Mrs Riley said. "We were very sorry to hear about what happened to your aunt and your mother. How are they?"

Mrs Riley moved forward as if to go into the house, but Ruthie remained slumped in the doorway.

"They're okay," she said, her voice flat and hollow. She brought them up to date as if she were reading from a medical report, then stopped when all the facts had been delivered. She did not invite the Rileys in.

"Is there anything you need?" Mrs Riley asked, her brow furrowed with concern.

"No, thank you," Ruthie replied. "I'm just fine."

"Are you sure you wouldn't like to spend the night with us?"

"No, thank you."

"Well, I'd like to visit your mother in the hospital."

Ruthie began to speak, stopped to clear her throat, then started over again. "They . . . um . . . the doctor said family only, Mrs Riley. But I'll tell her you stopped by."

"Oh. Well, I certainly don't want to impose. You *will* let us know if there's anything we can do?"

"Sure. And thanks. Bye. Bye, Denise." Backing into the house, Ruthie quietly shut the door. Mrs Riley stared for a moment at the spot Ruthie had occupied, then turned towards Denise, her mouth open with an unformed question. Denise looked away, guilty at knowing more than she could tell her mother, but utterly confused by Ruthie's withdrawn behaviour. The face and voice were at once Ruthie's and those of a total stranger. Slowly, it dawned on

Denise that no matter how close their friendship grew, there would always be places, deep within Ruthie, that she would never be able to go. The realisation made her tremble with a kind of awe. How complicated people could be! It was all too much, she thought, suddenly feeling very young and helpless, way too much for her to handle all alone.

Safe in her mother's car, Denise longed to unburden herself of everything she knew about Ruthie. She knew Ruthie might hate her for it. But the girl she had just seen was not the Ruthie she knew, but a ghostly creature who was refusing help she obviously needed.

"That was very strange," Mrs Riley observed, steering the car carefully through the darkened streets.

"What was?"

"She didn't ask us in. She acted as if she hardly even recognised us."

"Yeah. I guess."

"Maybe I ought to call her aunt. I don't know. Maybe not. She knows everyone in town. She's probably besieged with calls. What do you think?"

Denise shrugged helplessly, a huge lump swelling in her throat.

The street lights were on when Mrs Riley pulled up in front of their house. She turned off the motor, but made no move to get out of the car. Denise also sat still, very still, waiting, battling with herself, wanting to talk but afraid to. For a long while, Mrs Riley stared out the window, absently running a finger back and forth along her lower lip. Then, she turned and covered Denise's hand with her own.

"I think you'd better tell me the whole story," she said.

"Yeah," Denise agreed, hoarsely. "I guess so."

And it all gushed out of her, filling the night air with secrets, from the grizzly buried photographs to the arrogance of Maxine Fitzhugh.

"And if that oversexed creep says one word to Ruthie tomorrow," Denise concluded, "*one word*, I swear I don't know what I'll do. I won't be responsible for my behaviour, that's for sure."

Mrs Riley stroked Denise's hair soothingly. "Oh, Pumpkin, Pumpkin," she crooned, "never a dull moment. *When* will you understand you can't save the world all alone? You can't right all the wrongs all the time all by yourself. No one human being is that powerful."

"Then what *should* we do," Denise wailed, "just let people suffer and die? Just go on as if nothing bad ever happened? Terrible things happen all the time, everywhere. What are we supposed to do? Nothing? Just let them happen?"

"Denise, listen to me," Mrs Riley insisted, "it's not all black and white. It's not fix-it-all-right-this-minute or fix nothing ever. Real life is somewhere in between. Real life is doing what you can—and not giving up if it falls short of perfection."

"But what can I do for Ruthie? She's so unhappy. It's not fair!"

"I know it's not fair, but that's the way things are sometimes. And all you can do right now is to go on being her friend."

"That's not enough!"

"But it's a *lot*."

"I want her to be happy."

"She will be. But nobody's happy all the time."

Denise gasped, recognising her mother's words as a thought she'd had herself, not long ago. Ruthie had wanted *her* to be happy all the time and, of course, that was impossible.

"Remember the prayer I gave you a while ago?" Mrs Riley asked. " 'God, grant me the courage to change the things I can change, the serenity to accept those I cannot change, and the wisdom to know the difference.' Remember that?"

Denise thought it over. Maybe, just *maybe*, it was beginning to make a little bit of sense. For the moment, she'd wait and see.

Maxine couldn't say anything to Ruthie the next day, because Ruthie didn't show up for school. Her absence threw Denise into a panic that threatened to gnaw a hole through her stomach wall by three o'clock.

The only thing that stood between Denise and total hysteria was the peculiar behaviour of her classmates. When she arrived, a bunch of them were huddled around her desk, Maxine and Betsy at the centre of the knot. Denise froze when they all turned to face her, with expressions so serious she couldn't tell what they were about to do.

"Where's Ruthie?" Maxine asked.

"Isn't she here yet?" Denise said, through clenched teeth.

The circle of heads shook in unison. Denise waited, tensed for some kind of nasty blow.

"We were really sorry about what happened to her aunt and her mother," Maxine went on. The faces behind her bobbed in agreement. "A lot of people think it had something to do with my father. That maybe he even threw the rock. But he felt terrible about it. Honest, Denise, it really shook him up. He and my mother spent half the night at Sarah Abrams' house."

"I thought they were enemies," Denise said, trying to figure out what the trick was. Why was Maxine being so nice all of a sudden? Or was she really as scared and concerned as she looked?

"They *disagree*," Maxine said, quietly. "That doesn't make them enemies. My dad says that Ruthie's aunt doesn't take into account the fact that building those houses would give a lot of people work who desperately need it. And building them inexpensively would give people homes who can't afford the best of everything. He says there's more than one way to look at the problem. And that Mrs Abrams is an idealist. He says she's a good, honest woman, but not

105

always reasonable. But he would never hurt her, Denise. In fact, he even *voted* for her. He is afraid, though, that it might have been one of his employees who threw the rock. A lot of them really need the work."

Denise chewed her lower lip. It was all much too confusing. The bad guys weren't all that bad; the heroine was less than perfect; friends could be distant sometimes and enemies could be kind. She had a lot of thinking to do.

All through the day, the class stuck close to Denise, Maxine the closest of all, as if to protect her. They fretted over Ruthie's absence almost as much as she did. They packed themselves into the principal's office to huddle around the phone when she tried to call Ruthie before lunch, and groaned when there was no answer. Denise could hardly believe it. Beneath all their silly quibbling and jealousies, they really cared about her and Ruthie.

But *caring* wasn't enough, not for a best friend, anyway. There had to be some way she could help Ruthie. A best friend couldn't just stand by and watch someone suffer. There just *had* to be something she could do. But what? She was stacking her dishes and tray when the answer finally hit her.

"Okay! Okay!" she cried to no one in particular, "So maybe I can't help. But I can get someone who can!" And back to the office she ran to make one last phone call.

The day was nearly over when somebody remembered the Sigma Iota Spring Fling.

"Oh, yeah," Maxine said. "I won."

"How come you're not shouting it from the rooftops?" Denise wondered.

"Oh, I will," Maxine said, "but this isn't the right time for it."

Her smile, amazingly shy for Maxine, was actually pretty, Denise thought. She couldn't be absolutely sure, but she was beginning to suspect that Maxine's popularity was not entirely due to her 32B.

14

Ruthie lay motionless in bed and watched her alarm clock move its hands with mesmerising regularity past the time for school to begin, then past home ec., maths, English and lunch. Twice the phone rang, long and loudly, but she didn't answer it. She couldn't. There was nothing left of her, no will, no strength. She knew she should visit her mother, check up on her aunt, call the rabbi or Mrs Riley or someone. But instead she lay like a crushed doll on the bed, limp and hopeless, watching the minutes tick by. The clock ticked away the new life she had hoped for, the life of sunshine and joy Denise had shown her. It was all gone now, collapsed beneath her load of grief and pain. Only the empty minutes were left.

At about the time gym would be starting, with the clanging of locker doors and the smell of sweaty sneakers and talcum powder, Ruthie heard someone pounding on the front door. Her heartbeat quickened, surprising her; she really thought it had stopped beating altogether. Prickles of fear tingled along her neck and hands, the first feeling since she'd awakened. Slowly, weakly, she pulled herself out of bed and struggled towards the living room window. From there, she could see the figure beating on the front door. It was Rabbi Davis. With a little cry, Ruthie ran to the door and opened it.

His kind, loving face and the warmth of the sun behind it seemed to flood her entire body.

"Your friend, Denise, thought you might need me," he

said. Then he held out his arms and Ruthie fell into them. For a long time, he held her and rocked her like a baby, while her tears soaked his shirt in an ever-widening dark stain.

When she was finally able to speak, she blurted out, "I can't be bat mitzvahed, Rabbi. I'm too afraid. I know Aunt Sarah will be terribly hurt, but it's too much to ask. I can't stand up in front of everyone and be Jewish. Not after everything that's happened. Maybe my father was right. Maybe they won't hate us anymore if we don't even exist."

Rabbi Davis led Ruthie to the sofa where they sat close to each other, her fragile little hand in his large, bony one.

"Is that what your father thought?"

"I don't know. Probably. It seemed that way to me. Oh, I don't know. I just don't know."

"But we do exist, Ruthie; for better or worse, here we are. Your father existed, too, whatever he thought."

Ruthie rubbed her aching head with her free hand, and sighed miserably. "I'm so mixed up. There's Aunt Sarah's way of looking at it, too. That my bat mitzvah is some sort of triumph over our enemies, that I have to go through with it, make a big show of it, just to prove to them we're still here. But Aunt Sarah is *strong*, she can do things like that. She doesn't care what people think. In fact, the more people disagree with her, the stronger she gets. I'm not like her. She's a . . . a *warrior*. And I'm weak and scared. Only, well, sometimes I think maybe she's right. At least I know part of me wants so much to please her. You should have seen her dancing around the kitchen when I said okay. But look at what she went through yesterday. How would I take it, being insulted and hurt for what I believed in? How would I stand it? I can't even stand it now and nobody's thrown rocks at me. At least, not yet. Oh, I don't know what I want, Rabbi."

"What does your mother have to say about all this?"

"That's the worst of all. I don't know what she thinks. I

don't know what she thinks about *anything*. She never shares the least little thing about herself with me."

"Maybe she's afraid to, Ruthie."

"Afraid? Of *me*?"

"No, not of you. But perhaps your mother feels that the less she hopes for in life, the less she cares about anything, the less she can be hurt."

A shock of recognition reverberated inside Ruthie. Yes! That was it! That explained so much of her mother's behaviour, her secrecy, her distance. How much did the rabbi know about her mother? And who had told him?

"Your aunt has filled me in on a lot of your mother's background," he said, as if reading her thoughts, "so I kind of understand her problems, as much as anyone could who hasn't had to endure what she's been through. On the other hand, nobody's really filled me in on *you*, Ruthie, not even you, yourself. I see you often, we talk; many times, I feel you're troubled. But I can't even begin to guess what's going on inside your altogether too serious little head. If you want to tell me, though, now or any other time, I'll always be ready to listen."

Still clutching his hand as if to let go meant to fly off the face of the earth, Ruthie led the way to her mother's room and took out the locket and the box of photographs. Having once told Denise everything that had haunted her since childhood, she found this second telling far easier. Would her confession cause another horrible nightmare tonight? It didn't matter anymore. She could live through a nightmare. She'd lived through all the others. And somehow, she sensed, letting out the secret miseries of her soul lessened their power to devastate her.

Rabbi Davis listened quietly, a hint of tears glimmering in his eyes, as Ruthie explained what she'd heard about her parents' past and what she'd guessed or imagined to fill in the wide, troubling gaps in the story.

"I want to make my mother happy, to see her cheerful

and hopeful like Denise's mother and father. I want to make them all happy, my parents and Aunt Sarah and all the ghosts of the dead I carry around with me. But I can't. I don't know how. I don't even know what they want. I don't even know what *I* want. Does that make any sense at all?"

Rabbi Davis pursed his lips thoughtfully. "Yes," he said, at last, nodding his head. "I'm afraid it does."

The rabbi made several phone calls, then scrambled a few eggs for Ruthie and himself. Together, they waited while Aunt Sarah picked up Ruthie's mother at the hospital and brought her home. When the familiar Continental pulled up in front of the house, Ruthie and Rabbi Davis were standing side by side in the doorway, ready to greet them. Waves of anxiety washed over Ruthie. She knew what had to be done now, but wasn't at all sure she had the strength to do it. She took what comfort she could from the rabbi's lanky presence at her side.

"Well, here we are," Aunt Sarah announced. "A little worse for the wear, but we'll survive."

Ruthie's mother smiled shyly and pecked her on the cheek. Her tests had been negative and she actually looked healthier than usual after her night of drug-enforced rest.

"Hello, Mama," Ruthie said. "Are you all right?"

Mrs Morgenthau nodded, but said nothing.

"They gave her one last shot, to keep her relaxed," Aunt Sarah explained. She helped settle Mrs Morgenthau on the sofa, then took the dark, bulky easy chair for herself, plopping deep into its cushions so that her feet, like a child's, barely touched the floor. She'd arranged what was left of her hair so that the bandage was almost covered. Perfectly groomed once again, she looked refreshed and ready for the next challenge.

Ruthie sat on the floor beside her mother and the rabbi brought a straight-backed chair in from the kitchen for himself.

"Such *tsuris*, such trouble, we don't need," Aunt Sarah announced. "It makes me furious. That rotten sneak, to attack me like that, not even face to face like a *mensch*. You see, Ruthie, *you see* why you must be bat mitzvahed and why it must be a huge celebration, in front of everybody, loud and joyous and strong? We will show them we are not afraid, we will not be intimidated, we will never again march to the slaughterhouses like lambs. Enough is enough. Do you see now?"

Ruthie flinched before the force of Aunt Sarah's determination. Imploringly, she looked towards the rabbi for help. He was folding and unfolding his hands nervously. He seemed deep in thought, as if weighing the wisdom of what he was about to do. He stuttered over his words at first.

"Sarah," he said, at last, "there is something—there are many things we must discuss. I know you've had a hard couple of days, you and Hannah both. But I don't think this can wait any longer. And Hannah's medication may be to our advantage. When I came here today, Ruthie was a hopeless little heap of confusion and exhaustion, truly on the verge of nervous collapse. She had given her all for you and for her mother, because you needed her. But in doing so, she used herself up, drained herself, almost did herself real, perhaps irreparable, harm. She needs you now, your patience and your understanding. And first and foremost, she needs your honesty."

"Our honesty?" Aunt Sarah exclaimed. "When have we not been honest?"

"You were never knowingly dishonest, Sarah, I'm sure. But what you are unaware of is this: on the many nights when you and Hannah discussed what had happened in Germany during the war, Ruthie was hiding in the hallway, listening."

Mrs Morgenthau and Aunt Sarah gasped, then turned towards Ruthie in disbelief. Ruthie bowed her head, unable to meet their incredulous eyes, wishing the rabbi would stop, but knowing he couldn't.

"She heard only part of what was said," he went on, quietly, calmly, but with an undertone of urgency to his voice, "and being very young, she understood even less. Her whole being was then filled with questions and not one of them has ever been answered."

"We were protecting her," Aunt Sarah broke in. "What does a child need to know of such atrocities?"

"I understand. You thought it was best. But instead of the truth, Ruthie's lived with a child's worst imagined fears, not of what *really* happened, but of what *might* have happened. An infinity of horrors, like the distorted mirrors in a haunted house that go on and on without end. Believe me, reality, no matter how ugly, is preferable to that."

Aunt Sarah tried to speak again, but, moving almost in slow motion, Ruthie's mother raised a hand to stop her.

"The rabbi is right," she said.

Aunt Sarah protested. "Hannah, you don't have to talk. Please. You don't have to put yourself through this."

"Ruthie needs to know the truth."

"Then let *me* tell her."

But Mrs Morgenthau shook her head, with the quiet immovable stubbornness Ruthie knew so well. "In my heart, I have always known this day would come. But I never had the courage for it. Very well, it is here, courage or no. I must tell her the truth. But please understand, Ruthie, it is very difficult for me. And some things, perhaps some details, I will still leave out. There is much I have forgotten, except in my dreams."

As Mrs Morgenthau paused to gather her memories, the room grew so quiet, Ruthie could hear herself breathe. She looked at her mother and felt suddenly shy, as if they were strangers.

"First, I know you have seen the locket."

Ruthie's mouth fell open in surprise.

"Once, in the old house, I happened to come upon you looking at it. I couldn't bring myself to talk to you about it then. As with everything else, I tried to pretend it had not happened. But now, I must face it . . . with you." Mrs Morgenthau faltered and turned her face away from Ruthie as she blinked back tears. "Her name was Rachel," she continued, softly, "perhaps you already know that, too. She was your half-sister."

"Half-sister?"

"Yes. I was married before I met your father."

"Hannah, please . . ." Aunt Sarah broke in, her face contorted with pained concern for her sister-in-law. But Mrs Morgenthau went on.

"I married my, as they say, childhood sweetheart. In fact, I was still a child, only seventeen years old. We had only a few years together. Then we were arrested and deported to concentration camp. My husband and I were separated. I never saw him again. I was sent to a labour camp, I suppose because I had been a seamstress and they found that a useful skill. My husband, Abraham, was a scholar and a teacher, so gentle the children rushed to school each morning and hung on his arms long after they should have gone home. His were talents for which the Nazis had no use.

"I arrived in camp, holding my little Rachel, a woman and child half-dead already, because Abraham was half of our lives, half of our souls. Your father, Ruthie, David Morgenthau, spotted me in the first minute and saved my life. He was a tailor and convinced the Nazis I was an excellent seamstress and that he would be personally responsible for my productivity. He was an amazing man, strong and stubborn in spite of his imprisonment. Even they, the madmen, who respected nothing human, were, I think, a little in awe of him.

"He guided me, a dazed animal, through the endless days and nights. We made their uniforms, God forgive us, and for that they fed us just enough to keep us from starving to

113

death. Your father and I shared everything with Rachel, but it wasn't enough. Like so many, many others, she contracted dysentery and, day by day, night by terrifying night, she grew weaker and weaker until she died. She was not quite five years old."

Mrs Morgenthau paused. The room had filled with a sadness so heavy, it was far beyond tears.

"After that, I no longer really existed. I felt nothing; I cared for nothing. I did what David told me to do, and he even had to tell me to eat and to sleep. And so, together, we survived. Survived! All his energy, all his magnificent strength and dignity, he concentrated on our survival. Like the sun's heat intensified through a magnifying glass, he burned our way through it all. No, Ruthie, I was not tortured, I was not beaten. Not in the physical sense, anyway. But others were, Jews and gentiles alike. I saw it and I survived. And there are days—and especially nights—when I can stand my memories no longer and I wish your father had let me perish with my family, with Abraham and Rachel, and my parents and my grand-parents. Twelve million people, six million of them Jews. Numbers! What do they mean? Little families, they mean, husbands and wives, mamas and babies, uncles, aunts, cousins. And friends. All gone. And I survived. Because of your father, Ruthie, a man who burned so brightly with the flame of life, it was enough for two.

"Well. After the Allies liberated us, we searched for my husband and learned of his fate. He was gassed to death at Auschwitz. I married your father, because, as with everything else, he decided it was best. Please try to understand, Ruthie, after all I'd been through, love was out of the question. We needed each other and so we stayed together. We came to America because your Uncle Izzy and Aunt Sarah were able to bring us here.

"But your father could never adjust to the fact that here, in America, he was dependent on his brother-in-law. Even in concentration camp, he had remained his own man. Here, without the language, without an understanding of this way of life, he felt displaced. And, he grew bitter. By the time you were born, Ruthie, he was a different man; his great passion for life had turned into hatred and anger."

"Izzy tried so hard to help him out," Aunt Sarah mused, "but the more he did, the more David resented him. It got so bad that they could not be in a room together. I visited your parents many times alone. You know that, Ruthie."

Ruthie nodded, the memory of the two women huddled at the kitchen table flickering across her mind.

"His dignity," Mrs Morgenthau murmured. "His dignity. What the war and the Nazis couldn't take from him, somehow a free country and a brother-in-law's charity did. Life, *vay iss mer*, life is very strange. But, Ruthie, one thing, perhaps, is important to remember. When you knew him, he was old and broken; but in his prime he was a man who valued life and fought for it, for himself, for me and for you."

Suddenly, Ruthie was on her knees by her mother's side, hugging her as she had never hugged her before. It was a horrible story, a heartbreaking story, but at least it was out. Now she could face it. She could begin to understand. It couldn't grab at her in the dark anymore, like a thousand faceless phantoms.

"Life," Aunt Sarah echoed, raising a finger as she readied herself to launch into a speech, "life is what the bat mitzvah is all about. Isn't that right, Rabbi? We celebrate each stage of life, birth, bat mitzvah, confirmation, marriage. Even at death, we say a prayer in praise of life. We go on. We must go on. Especially we three, the nucleus of a martyred family."

"We go on," the rabbi agreed, passing Ruthie his handkerchief to dry her tears, "but Sarah, we cannot go on making martyrs."

"What do you mean?"

"I mean, *Ruthie*. She was not even born when all these things happened to your family, and yet she's suffered, too. This is a new realisation, you know, just surfacing here and in Israel and wherever the survivors of the Holocaust settled. Their children carry a hidden burden. Like all children, they love their parents and want to please them. But they can never, ever make up for what their parents endured during the war. They cannot erase the past and they cannot live their lives as some kind of vengeance against the evils of the earth. That is too great a burden for anyone, but especially for a child. Ruthie has spent so much of her life trying to be what everyone else wants her to be, she doesn't even know what she wants herself. And she must find out, because Ruthie is Ruthie. She's not her friend, Denise; she's not you, Hannah, and she's not you, Sarah. Nor is she Rachel or Abraham or David, may their souls rest in peace. She's Ruthie, and whatever that means, we must let her find out for herself."

"Does that mean no bat mitzvah?" Aunt Sarah wondered.

"It means wait and see. One thing I know for sure about Ruthie: she is a good, loving person. She cannot save the world for us, but her very presence makes it worth saving. And Ruthie, remember this, no matter what you do, it will be good. And every good life, even the least dramatic, the least remarkable, the least visibly heroic, is a triumph over evil."

15

Denise leaped out of bed and ran to her window. The Saturday of Ruthie's bat mitzvah had dawned in a glorious burst of sunshine, she noted gleefully. It was perfect as only a June morning could be.

Before washing, before *anything*, Denise doublechecked her wardrobe. The dress she had bought for the morning services and the gown, her first ever, for the dinner dance were still there, another miracle. They were so grown-up, they made her look at least eighteen. Well, sixteen, for sure. She'd even relented and bought a bra, observing that it definitely made an interesting difference in the way the clothes hung on her body—which was suddenly, overnight, it seemed, slimmer. Well, not slimmer *everywhere*. Move over, Maxine Fitzhugh!

Then there was her new haircut to inspect. Had it survived another night? She bobbed and twisted in front of the dresser mirror, fluffing her curls with her fingertips. God, who *was* that sophisticated young woman? she wondered happily.

"Denise! Your *hair!*" Maxine had screamed, the minute she'd appeared in class Friday morning. Maxine and the other girls had clustered around her, oohing and ahhing at Mr James's tonsorial triumph. The boys, Denise couldn't help but notice, hung back at their seats and smirked. But they were looking, no doubt about it, they were looking.

Would any of them ask her to dance tonight? Did she even dare hope for it to be Todd Jones? Not that it mattered, of course. But he would be taller than she would be in her new heels. In fact, he'd be the *only one* taller than she, unless Aunt Sarah's grandchildren from California were unusually big for third- and fourth-graders.

Oh, well, the evening was a long way off. First came the ceremony at the synagogue. How nervous Ruthie must be! She'd been a wreck for the last week, but a cheerful kind of wreck, smiling prettily as she answered question after question from their classmates, who'd come to school clutching their engraved invitations in awe, as if they'd come from the White House. Denise gave her pale green chiffon gown a last, loving stroke, and hurried to get ready.

The small, wood-panelled synagogue was already packed with Deerfieldians when the Rileys arrived and slipped into a back pew. Ruthie was sitting on a platform behind the pulpit, across from Rabbi Davis, who wore a white prayer shawl and cap. Denise waved to Ruthie, who smiled then bit her lip. Was she going to cry or laugh with nervousness? Denise wondered. She decided to try not to look at Ruthie too much. It was making her own stomach do roller-coaster flip-flops.

While the congregation buzzed with anticipation, Denise glanced around to see who was there. The Fitzhughs were on the far side, two aisles down. Fitzhugh's buildings had been declared safe by the building code inspector and, after the election, the northeast property had been sold to Fitzhugh Development Corporation. Aunt Sarah had conceded graciously by inviting the Rileys, the Morgenthaus, and the Fitzhughs to one of her scrumptious dinners and getting everybody properly acquainted. Denise could not believe how tiny Aunt Sarah really was; no matter how often Ruthie had described her, Denise still expected a giant. Nor could she believe how cheerful Aunt Sarah was, even in defeat. "You win some, you lose some," she'd declared with a wink, and toasted the Fitzhughs with champagne that tickled Denise's nose and made her sneeze, much to everyone's amusement.

Denise had just spotted Betsy and was searching for Todd's blond head when the rabbi stood up and a hush fell over the room.

The service began with readings from the Psalms; the rabbi alone at first, and then alternating with the congregation. Then, Ruthie joined him in opening the delicately carved wooden doors of the Ark, revealing the Torah. It was covered in crimson velvet and topped with an ornate silver crown. Denise's stomach lurched anxiously, but Ruthie didn't seem the least bit nervous. Then Denise remembered her words of a couple of weeks ago: "I've rehearsed and rehearsed so much, even if I faint, I'll probably go right on reciting my part!"

The rabbi and Ruthie alternated chanting in Hebrew and then translating the prayers of praise and gratitude for the Torah and its teachings:

"Ba-re-chu et A-do-nai ha-me-vo-rach!" Praise the Lord to whom our praise is due!

"Barach A-do-nai ha-me-vo-rach le-o-lam va-ed!" Praised be the Lord to whom our praise is due, forever and ever!

After the Torah had been tenderly divested of its crown and cover, it was unrolled across the pulpit. One by one, men from the congregation came up to say a blessing over it. Between the blessings, Ruthie read the Hebrew scriptures and translated them into English. Denise recognised the Old Testament portion she was reading; it was about Moses receiving the Ten Commandments. Only once did Ruthie stumble over a word, and then the rabbi was right there to help her along. Ruthie herself recited the final blessing. Like the Torah reading itself, she had explained to Denise, that was an honour allowed only to adults in the Jewish community.

After more readings and prayers, Ruthie stepped to the

pulpit to begin her speech. This, she had confessed, was the hardest part of all, to gather her feelings about this momentous occasion and express them in her own words in front of everyone.

"Beloved Rabbi, Mama, Aunt Sarah, and dear friends," she began. She blinked several times and Denise crossed her fingers in her lap, all of them, including her thumbs. After a deep breath, Ruthie continued:

"This day marks the beginning of my adulthood according to Jewish law. From now on, I am responsible for my actions, my decisions, my physical and spiritual well-being. I know this will not be easy, because a couple of months ago, I was faced with the decision of whether or not even to have a bat mitzvah, and it was very hard. But I have learned that hard things, difficult and painful things, help us to grow. Through them, we increase our wisdom and understanding. By avoiding them, we get nowhere.

"This is supposed to be a joyous occasion, a celebration of life. After all my family had suffered, I wondered if there was a point in rejoicing. Was it even *right*? Sometimes I felt sure it was not right. There could be no more joy after such incredible pain. Other times, I thought, yes, we must go on, louder and stronger than before, to show that we're not defeated. But most of the time, I didn't know which way to go. In fact, most of this spring was spent going around in circles."

Ruthie smiled and the congregation chuckled softly in response. Denise felt the muscles of her stomach relax at last. She glanced sideways at her mother, so pretty in her new beige dress, and received a cheering wink.

"I circled around," Ruthie went on, "going over and over my past and my possible future and all that they meant and could mean. And, at last, with the help of Rabbi Davis, my mother, my Aunt Sarah, and my friends the Rileys, difficult things finally became simple and puzzling things became clear. First of all, I realised, I am alive. This is a fact.

And I'm alive because of my parents, my aunt and uncle, and God. And, for the same reasons, I am Jewish. And, for still the same reasons, I am very lucky. My history goes back beyond the Holocaust to many other persecutions, and to many other triumphs over them. Yes, I have suffered the pain of my ancestors. But I am also strong with their enduring strength. My parents were survivors. I'm a survivor, too. We all are, because any evil hurts more than its immediate victims; it hurts the human race.

"But we have survived. We are alive and there is a lot to celebrate. I, personally, celebrate today the love and determination of my parents and my aunt and uncle, who gave me life and brought me to this moment of adulthood. And I celebrate the friendship of Mr and Mrs Riley and Denise, who showed me something very new: how warm and full of fun life could be when you share it with loving friends. And I celebrate the patient teaching of Rabbi Davis, who helped me to see the value, the importance of my existence. Every good life, he told me not long ago, is a triumph over evil. Well, I am here, I am alive, and I am grateful. And my first adult promise is to try my very best to lead a good life. It will be hard, sometimes, I know. It will sometimes be painful. But it will be worth it. *L'chaim*, as my Aunt Sarah is so fond of shouting, *to life!*"

Denise's throat ached, but she didn't care. She wanted to applaud wildly, but remembered where she was just in time, and settled, instead, as did the rest of the congregation, for a tearfully happy smile, beaming her love and pride towards Ruthie.

The service concluded quickly with a blessing from the rabbi and soon the aisle was mobbed with friends wanting to congratulate Ruthie. Denise and her parents waited at their seats while the hubbub slowly diminished. Soon, no one was left in the synagogue except Ruthie, her mother, Aunt Sarah, and the Rileys. They stood bunched in the aisle, oddly shy and grinning, speechless with emotion.

Then, Ruthie and Denise were together, hugging and crying and jumping up and down. It crossed Denise's mind, only for a second, that this was probably not the most adult thing Ruthie could be doing.

The Willowtree Ballroom was aglow with candlelight and fresh flowers. Denise tottered in on her heels and decided it didn't matter if she was asked to dance or not. This was the most beautiful room she'd ever been in in her entire life and that was enough for her.

"Do they have cigarettes in those little cups on the tables?" Betsy piped up from behind her. She, Denise, Ruthie, and Maxine had just emerged from a last-minute checkup in the ladies' room.

"Of course not," Ruthie told her. "Aunt Sarah would be the last hostess in the world to *encourage* smoking."

"Oh," Betsy moaned. It was obvious to Denise that she'd stuffed something down the front of her hot-pink gown, something definitely lopsided. Poor old Betsy. Being Maxine's best friend must be hard on her.

"There are the guys," Maxine observed, nodding towards a huge round table where Todd Jones and his gang were flipping dinner mints into the air and catching them in their gaping mouths. "That's the kiddies' table, I suppose," Maxine sighed. "And there are four empty chairs, waiting for guess who?"

Denise's heart pounded as their little group approached the table and examined the place-cards. Hers was next to Todd. She shot Ruthie an accusing glare. Ruthie pretended not to notice, but she was smiling.

"Hi," Todd offered, as Denise slid as gracefully as possible into the seat beside him. Too late, she realised her dress was bunched up under her and would probably be creased beyond repair. Should she get up and smooth it? No. A gesture like that would look idiotic, maybe even obscene.

She tried to sit lightly to minimize the creases. In seconds, her back began to ache.

"Hi," she said, smiling in spite of everything. Immediately at a loss for words, Denise was thankful to see a fruit cocktail being placed before her. She busied herself with a melon ball while the band began to play, their volume eliminating the need for conversation.

"Wanna dance?" Todd practically screamed into her ear.

Her mouth full of melon ball, Denise glanced around the table. All eyes were on her, filled with envy, admiration, and/or amusement, depending on whose eyes they were. Chewing frantically, she nodded, and in a moment was off the lump on her dress and teetering towards the bandstand behind Todd Jones, who was a good two inches taller than her, high heels and all.

I will not trip, I will not trip, Denise sang to herself as she munched her melon and crossed the slick ballroom floor. I will not twist an ankle, I will not break my leg.

It was a slow dance, Denise noted. Was that good or bad? Good, because there was less chance of bodily harm; bad, because Todd had to put his arm around her and she wasn't sure she could take that. She'd also have to put her slightly sweaty hand into his. Surreptitiously, she wiped it off between the folds of her dress.

"Nice party," Todd observed.

They were dancing. Yes! They were actually dancing. Denise was sure of it, because the room was swimming around her. On the other hand, she was not quite sure she was breathing. She gulped down the last of her melon ball. Between that and the challenge of staying off Todd's toes, she doubted she could manage a conversation.

"Mmmmm-hmmmm," she said, and regretted it immediately. A dribble of melon juice was oozing out the side of her mouth. Both of her hands were occupied, or maybe paralysed, permanently clinging to Todd's left hand and right shoulder. She licked at the drop, pretending to cough slightly, so she could turn her head away. She felt her left toe graze the tip of his shoe and coughed harder by way of excuse.

"Are you okay?" Todd asked.

"Oh, sure. Little frog in my throat." The words sounded so silly, Denise felt a giggle rising in her chest. Oh, Lord, she didn't want to giggle. Giggling was so *childish*. But the harder she tried to stop, the funnier everything got. She kept picturing a tiny little frog tap-dancing merrily in her throat. With a little top hat and a wee silver cane. Rrrrribit! Rrrrribit!

"Something wrong?" Todd asked.

As he and Denise swung around, a gaggle of Rileys and Morgenthaus came into view. They were all watching Denise, with huge grins splitting their faces.

"Oh, no," Denise assured him. "Everything's fine, just fine."

"That's good," Todd said, a little huffily. "I thought you were laughing."

"Me? Laughing? Well, maybe just a bit."

"At what?"

"Oh, I don't know."

"At me?"

"Oh, no. Really, not at you."

"Then what?"

"I don't know. Well . . . at life, I guess. Yeah, that's it. *L'chaim!*"